PEACE *by* PIECE

PEACE *by* PIECE

DANCING IN THE LIGHT OF SPIRITUAL TRUTH
BEYOND DIAGNOSIS

BRITTANY C. HINES

Peace by Piece

First edition.

ISBN 13: 978-1-7352378-2-4

An ebook version of this book is also available:
ISBN 13: 978-1-7352378-4-8

Book cover design: Elena Karoumpali

Back cover photograph of Brittany: Noel Estevez

www.brittanychines.com

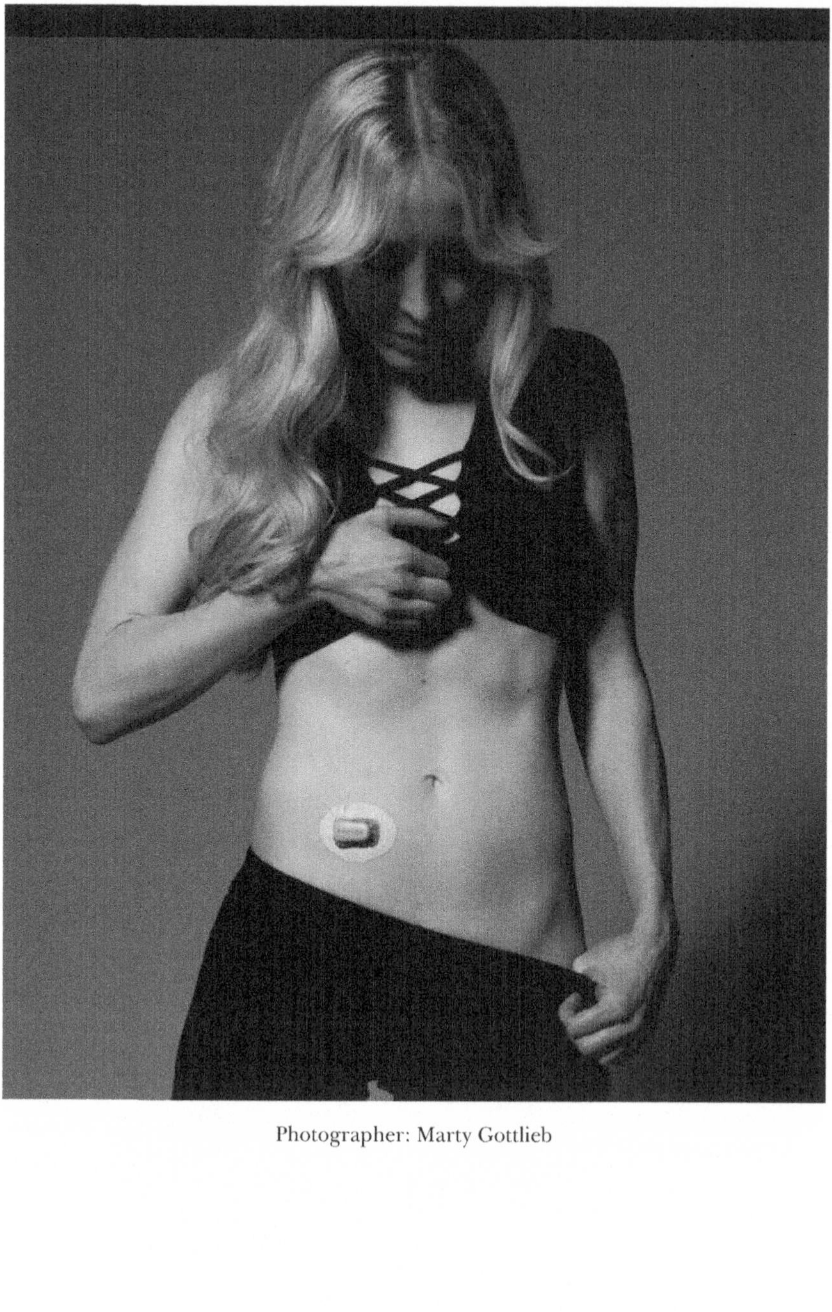

Photographer: Marty Gottlieb

Dedication

Thank you, Mom. For always telling me that happiness comes from the inside. Finally, I believe you.

I would like to wholeheartedly thank my mom, Yvonne Moroch, for truly *being* love toward me and showing me life through her warmest compassion. I thank my dad for the independence I learned at a tender age, which I would later use to propel me into achieving my ultimate level of success. Most of all, I thank God for making me whole again and for making *everything* possible—fulfilling me in mind, body, and spirit; guiding me to find true purpose in my life. I am forever grateful to the Light of this Universe for the Divine wisdom I have come to know. Most appreciatively, I would like to thank my family, friends, teachers, and doctors who have intentionally and unintentionally provided me with every bit of motivation to conquer my fears and inspire the world around me with who I *am*.

Contents

Preface

Welcome to my life, placed carefully and entertainingly into words. My name is Brittany Hines and I am a young, courageous woman living with Type 1 diabetes. The diagnosis at the age of 20 was quite a shock; I had such discipline for health and fitness. In a pea-sized capsule, like many of us, my childhood through adolescent days were filled with uncertainty, fear, and doubt. Fear of the future, fear of judgment, doubt in myself and my abilities in comparison to everyone around me, yet a smiling wallflower, from the heart, to all those who knew me.

Although I was timid in my younger years, to say the least, I knew I was holding myself back from living my best life. Still, I knew I was different and there was something unique about me that I had yet to experience with anyone else. Keeping this secret inside of me and showing only some parts of myself to the world, I hid from what I truly believed: that I was here for a reason. I acquired a dismissive attitude toward those who wanted to come close to me, closing myself off in my own little bubble of defeat—diabetes. It wasn't until March 9, 2008, on my deceased grandfather's birthday, that I would recognize my life to be reborn.

Nonetheless, I would later learn to appreciate this diagnosis as being sent by Divine destiny to push shy Brittany out of her comfort zone. Could it be? The quiet, rosy-cheeked little blonde-haired, blue-eyed Britt would learn of her strength through this disease? Well, it happened. And I'm here to share how I made life changing decisions, experienced a chock-full of laughter that served as my best medicine, and lived my most empowering days on a journey of healing, recovery, and restoration. Join me as I share my soul, open laughter, and Universal wisdom to flood the hearts of those who need it most...

Everyone.

Introduction

Have you ever noticed that in the waking moments of the morning, in which you are in solitude and of new breath, that the most active part of your being has already started planning your day while you lie motionless, glaring out to the messy blankets around you? Peeking with one slit of your eye open, it's as if an out-of-body experience occurs within just moments of waking—to let you know you're still *here*. You woke up today—and there's a Divine plan for you. Sounds great, right? Like, where do I sign up?

Well, the thing about this plan is that, regardless of what you may believe, you're going to show up. What happens to you thereafter is in large part due to the thoughts you restlessly gather in your mind as you push yourself up from your goose-filled pillow and smooth 1,000-thread-count sheets. Would you believe me if I told you that your happiness is a *choice*? Leave the cold coffee on the countertop, and let's delve into something your subconscious mind may not yet be aware of.

And so, I welcome you to the power of Today.

Your name here (Only WILLINGLY):

X ______________________________

CHAPTER ONE

Meeting Tomato

Before I woke up one morning, I had gone to bed with a plan of action for how to best use my time to accomplish all that I need to do to fulfill the dreams I had placed in my heart. We *all* have unique gifts that are placed within our mind and spirit; however, when these gifts will make themselves known is based entirely on just a few factors: willingness, receptiveness, and agreement. No one comes into this world with limits. However, through our experiences, conversations, and connections, we may unknowingly "take on" attributes that others feel suit us best. Soon, it's as if we are living at an address that we never agreed to move to. We quickly lose the sense of who we are because, unwittingly, we have tacked onto ourselves a slew of names and descriptions that our senses have picked up on along the way. Let me give you an example (I wasn't always such a conquistador!) By choice, I've made myself into the person I knew I had the power to be.

There once was a shy young girl; I knew her well growing up. She lived quietly, almost silently, observing, analyzing, and listening to the world around her. "Do you ever TALK!?" exclaimed one classmate. "Oh my goodness, she's in this class?" "Did anyone even know she was HERE?!" "Everybody look! She's turning red like a TOMATO!!" I would often hear this across the room. I always felt sorry for this friend of mine because she never truly seemed comfortable in her own skin, or around others. Her teachers seemed to embrace the very obvious "wallflower" that she exhibited—accepting, ignoring, and showing favor to those who appeared to have a more distinct voice. I guess this is when I learned that actions really do speak louder than words, and that the world will willingly take you as you "show up" that day. Looking back (because assessing what's behind you is imperative to the growth you embrace *today*), I don't recall "Lamb" (we'll call her) ever raising a hand, stating her views, or even striking up a conversation, as she had become so fearful. I watched Lamb take on the heaviness and demands of the girl that the world *wanted* her to be, up until about the age of 18.

Lamb was considered timid by those who knew her, afraid by those who judged her, boring by the risk-takers, slow by the teachers who failed to know and discover her strengths, and fragile by those who saw her well up with tears when working her hardest to just "get things right." Maybe you feel like you've met Lamb, but most likely you haven't. Lamb stayed away from the outer world—the chaotic New York streets, loud conversations, and social outings—because she didn't feel she was worthy of acceptance or love. The words she learned and overheard from those who were closest to her diminished her self-esteem, her sense of worth, and her capacity to show who she truly was for many, many years. I sometimes wonder how Lamb is today and who she "showed up" to be. I wonder if she genuinely loved the red cheeks that made her so beautiful. I wish she knew how special I thought she was, even then. If I ever cross paths with her again, I will tell her that because of her, I found the dreams inside myself.

CHAPTER TWO

Finding My Fingerprints

Someone very dear to me once told me that sometimes, the questions we ask ourselves and think about are more important than finding the answers. I reflect on this notion often because in my childhood I always had questions—and even *still* have a plethora of questions. I bet you do, too! As a matter of fact, we all do, rational or irrational, large or small; our brains are wired to constantly figure out the unknown. It's as if we are playing a real-life game of Monopoly in which we've configured and maneuvered every possible outcome in our mind. We strategize, plot, and ask questions, hoping to win the overall game, with little remembrance of or care paid to the important choices we make along the way.

Life, I've learned, is a journey with a lot of pit stops, not one final dream destination. We must contemplate the questions we often ask and consider...are we *prepared* to know the *authentic* answer? Maybe we are better off with some things left unexplained. Maybe the closure we seek so often is really just a stepping stone to discovering who we *really* are. Perhaps, if the answers to all that we ponder were spelled out for us, the greatest mysteries of life would not be worth living. Hear me out...but, sometimes it is in our greatest difficulties that we are pushed to do things outside our comfort zone or our realm of knowing. I choose to believe that there is something greater inside each and every one of us. Despite what we consider the "perfect" time or most trying time, there is *always* a level of power and Divine consciousness floating around us that supplies our intuition, guides us, and provides us with messages to enjoy and consider along the way. This connection is what shapes our life experience as we know it. Let me introduce you to the person whom I chose to observe and know the most: Lamb.

Meet the authentic fingerprint of "Lamb" (yep! that's me!)—a wonderful nickname my mother and grandpa brewed up as I shied away from celebrating my first double-digit birthday in the Miami sunshine. At ten years old, I didn't know much about why I felt uncomfortable in my own skin. I didn't question why I felt ashamed of who I was. I didn't want to talk about why I was shy and unengaged or celebrate the cautious kid I was. I just moved through each moment, day in and day out, enjoying myself and my family—in a quiet, reserved way, rather than in a fully present, open, and expressive way. Don't get me wrong, I had a huge appreciation for my mom and grandparents' going out of their way for me—decadent Cadbury's chocolate bars stacked to the top of the pantry shelf; the crispiest, juiciest apples that needed two hands to bite into; the seashells that I freely collected as I took serene walks with my grandparents along the shore. They gave me love, brought me joy, and spent meaningful time with me. I had it *all*...but I didn't *see* it. There was abundance all around me...love *all* around me...but, why didn't I feel it within myself? Acknowledging that my family wanted to continuously celebrate me and that I felt a desire to "conserve" who I was, my likes, dislikes, and all that I stood for, I grew increasingly independent and passive in my daily life.

"What do you want to do, Britt?"

"I don't care! Whatever you want to do."

"What TV show would you like to watch, Britt?"

"Doesn't matter to me! I like everything. I'll be happy watching something that makes you happy."

Excuse me!? Such a pleasant "Lamb" this sweet Britt was, but where was my sense of self? I had no backbone! No love for who I was. No confidence to express or declare that I mattered. I continued to live my life, peeping out of my invisible tortoise shell, slicing each wedge of Carvel ice cream cake each birthday, until I was nineteen. I remember blowing out the candles, wishing for happiness. "Please God, show me what I need to do to experience happiness. Help me to love myself from within..."

The dream was set. I was brave and bold enough to consign my intentions to the Universe. Soon after this particular birthday, while the energies of the Universe heard my desires, I would discover something life-changing, something that would transform who I was and help me to get in touch with what I was made for. "Maybe all those redundant, incessant questions I had were preparing me for this very moment," I thought. My fingerprints were quite literally and unexpectedly being pressed and found.

CHAPTER THREE

Some Piece of Cake...

"Brittany! Cooper pooped on the rug by the front door; can you help me clean it?" shouted Samantha, as I studied the shaggy dog who gave me grimacing, awfully obnoxious-for-an-animal looks every afternoon. I think he soon came to realize that I was the dual dog walker and babysitter whom he would begrudgingly welcome in his quiet abode at 3:00 on weekday afternoons.

"Sure, Sam! Let me give you a hand. I'll go grab some paper towels," I yelled. Just as I unraveled the thick Bounty roll that seemed to always do such a perfect job of a clean rip, I walked over the smudges on the multicolored rug and saw a nice wet one. "Man...this is great!" I thought. "Just yesterday, the freakin' dog escaped out the side door." As he ignored my calls to him, I heard the school bus roll around the corner and watched him *literally* tumble beneath the wheels. FYI: The dog almost put himself in his own doghouse! I tried to convince myself this chaotic event never happened, but it did. This, my friend, was with no exaggeration! One that could only happen with such a doofy, moody dog! "This dog's gotta go, or I gotta go," I whispered to myself. "I think it's time to get myself together and figure out my purpose. I mean, babysitting is great and all, but what am I really here for?" It had been three-and-a-half wonderful, easy-peasy years of straight couch-potato veggin', macaroni makin', and educatin' tweens on social ladder etiquette. But, I was not about to become a pro wiper for this downright delinquent, dirty dog! I'll just say, my babysitting no longer required the term "baby" in it, and it was time to move on!

As 6:00 rolled around one Friday evening in spring, I heard the jingle of keys that told me that Mr. and Mrs. Bailey had returned from their hard day at work. As I used two hands to push myself out of the butt socket I had created for my own fanny and assured the kids I could not wait to see them again next week, I smiled and headed toward the front door. Luckily, the poop smell was gone, and I was able to share a quick exchange of words with the family I had grown to love. "What are you doing tonight—anything special, Brittany?"

"Oh, yes! I'm actually very excited, my friends and I are going to be going dancing in New York City."

"Ah, how fun that will be! Although, you do look pale, Brittany. Much paler than usual...do you feel okay?" Mrs. Bailey inquired.

"Yeah! Oh, yeah. I can't *wait*. It will be so much fun, and I really look forward to seeing my friends and letting loose!" Mind you, I was never quite the party type—I loved to dance, loved to eat, but drinking and smoking were not my cup of tea.

After we hugged goodbye for the evening, I proceeded out the front door to my black Jetta. I was always eager and excited to rev the engine on this baby, even if just for a few blocks along the way, as it was my first car. "WEEEEEKEND!!!! HERE I COME!!!!" I exclaimed, as I turned the knob up to the highest volume and veered toward home.

As I ran up the what-seemed-like-forever cement steps to my door, I leaped with excitement for the night ahead. I had already picked out my outfit, designed my hairdo, and primed my fingernails to be ready for some sharp poking, should anyone break out a Macarena move or threaten my dance space, and I was *ready*.

"Want a slice of pizza, Britt? It's fresh and hot, we just ordered!" shouted my beautiful mom. (Mom and I have a distinct, over-the-moon type of love that can be seen and described immediately by anyone who comes into contact with us.) You can imagine the joy in my heart at the prospect of having a sit-down dinner with the woman I looked up to most, my knuckleheaded brother, and a cheesy, perfectly made pizza with as little crust as possible. Just as I like it!

Before I could even answer a hearty "OF COURSE!" a loud telephone ring ricocheted through the high ceilings and marble floors of our newly refinished kitchen.

My mom looked up at me and handed me the phone in a reassuring manner. "It's for you, Britt...it's Dr. Stern's office." Just a few days prior, I had gone for my routine checkup.

I walked toward the phone while every bit of childhood freedom and deliciousness sat still, waiting on the plate for me.

"Brittany? It's Dr. Stern's office. The bloodwork came back; your blood sugar is 616 you must get to your nearest emergency room, *IMMEDIATELY!*" the woman on the other end tried to annunciate all in one big breath.

I, a ripe somewhat naive twenty-year-old, had questions (as I typically would), retorting to this nonsense so to speak.

"Can I wait till I have my pizza? I was just about to eat dinner. Do I need to go right now?" Not fully understanding what *sugar* had to do with any of the time between my pizza that I so often ate and enjoyed like a normal child and my dancing plans, I thought I could just...wait. Surely, this would go away, and everything would be OK, again...*right?*

"No, go right now! Normal sugars are *much, much* lower," she tried to explain. "You could eat buckets and buckets of sugar and your numbers would never go as high as yours are right now!" She paused. "THIS IS AN EMERGENCY, BRITTANY! Your life is on the line!"

"But I ate a bunch of pasta today. Maybe, like, two bowls full! That's probably why. I'm sure it'll go away..."

"YOU NEED TO GO TO THE EMERGENCY ROOM AND SEE A DOCTOR, RIGHT AWAY. PLEASE!"

I hung up, shaking, slamming the phone onto the receiver. I

yelled and paced back and forth, from the kitchen table to the front door, explaining through my chattering teeth all that had been explained to me in the longest two minutes of my life. My mom and I dodged for the front door, pizza and brother holding the fort, while I panicked about the information I heard and tried to mentally prepare myself for the journey I was about to embark on.

We raced through traffic to get to the hospital and get right in. What we found first was a security man with a navy-blue hat and well-ironed uniform who nonchalantly came out to see who was here for the party and what in fact we were bringing to this party. "Nothing but a bag o' chips, a look of fear, and tears," I thought, as he smiled and hopped toward us. "EMERGENCY!" my mom blurted at him. The traffic czar lifted the gate and we were soon accepted into the place where I would find myself spending the loneliest of nights—three of them—filled with highly intense, almost dumbfounding information that my brain could not and did not want to process. My life was changing from this moment on...and I knew it. "Blood sugar - 415 - Admitted." I saw the entry official jot my information on her long list of questions in which I was robotically and systematically required to answer. I could feel the pit in my stomach. I feared what I knew not, but my intelligence served me; I knew, through all of my body's signals, that this was no ordinary visit. I blamed myself, as I cried through the night; I replayed everything I could have, should have, and would have done differently in my life to avoid this. I felt helpless, useless, cold, tired, and alone.

CHAPTER FOUR

Tuning into My Two Alarms

The night turned to morning as I woke up to the sounds of drips and beeps, coughing, and sneaker squeaks while nurses paced the floors of the emergency room. I tried to remember who I was...but, it was hard for me. My eyes were swollen from all of my tears while my body did everything it could to fight to stay alive and function. I watched as each nurse or attending doctor walked with urgency, coats swaying past the curtain, while carrying pills, trays of medical supplies, or clipboards of paperwork. I bit my nails, trying to control my nerves and fighting a stream of tears as I became more and more emotionally numb. As I write of that time in my life, now, I remember every little detail, as if it were yesterday. I find it quite amazing that despite the number of years that have passed since then, I remember every conversation, and every single phone call during my stay. But maybe that's the work of God and our mind. Maybe, a part of our life work is really, for us to learn how to *use* our mind to pay attention to and learn from the situations and events that shape every part of our being. As we may later recognize that this is what drives us to become who we are *meant* to become.

My experience in the hospital was nothing short of depressing. All that kept running through my mind is that one lame joke that typically comes up at a random house party or in front of a bonfire. "Hey! If you found out your life was over and you could only bring three things, what would they be?!" Yeah. I guess you could say my mind did everything it could to prepare for survival mode. There was this intense urgency to inform those that mattered to me that I needed them, or, hopefully, vice versa. I remember every phone call I was allowed to make, every person I spoke with in that period of time, and especially those who stood right by my side.

I was quite naive, as any twenty-something may be, and I convinced myself that the attending doctor for my case had *surely* made a misdiagnosis. "YOU'LL BE ON INSULIN THE REST OF YOUR LIFE. IF YOU DON'T TAKE YOUR MEDICINE, YOU'LL DIE!" the emergency room doctor exclaimed. Well, that was a surefire way to produce some tears, buddy. So cold and heartless—it was sad that this had become routine news for a doctor to blurt out, with no sensitivity chip installed. I tried to deny it. I tried to tell myself it would all be okay, but I didn't know who or what to believe. I didn't want to believe what I was hearing was actually true! "Is this because diabetes is on the rise and he's tired of meeting people like me?" I wondered. In and out, I watched the doctor zip and zag, on to the next patient. I was told of my diagnosis and then explained related things about diabetes that made me fear the rest of my days here on this planet. I couldn't help but feel like this life-changing experience was no more serious than a "Happy-Meal-to-go" for this "professional."

I watched as his lab coat flapped side-to-side, and in the blink of an eye I was on my own with nurses to discuss my care. I couldn't believe my eyes and my ears. But, I was certain that I would never make *anyone* feel discounted, the way I had felt in this one life-changing conversation. That could very well be the teacher in me—I always like to explain, or guide. Not this educated doctor—his method seemed tactless: tell and move on. I was never a fast food junkie...but, when I was a kid? Who didn't love the occasional drive-through? Still, those times were limited, as I was always health-conscious—and everyone knew it. I loved nothing more than crunching a juicy leaf of lettuce or a heaping fork of chickpea salad. Swim team, track star, dancer, orange belt with two stripes in karate—I mean, this girl was goin' places. Naturally, I was certain that this whole diabetes thing would just *go away* once they let me leave this lock-down area.

Convinced that I was still in control of what was happening, I remained tucked away in a curtained cubicle and Styrofoam reclining bed waiting for the big "Just kidding!" sign to pop up... but, it never did. I recall a nurse waking me from my sleep to prick my finger with a needle, late one evening. She came in with a little glucose meter, grabbed what looked like a mini-wand and said, "This might hurt a little." She must've known I was new to this blood sugar control thing, as I glanced at her perfectly manicured hair and a too-many-flowers scrub number on. Lying there confused and helpless, I observed every step the nurse performed as she carefully pulled the plunger and squeezed my finger, pushing for a blood droplet to squeeze out of my fragile fingertip. I watched her use my body in a way that made me feel as though I was taking part in an out-of-body experience, watching a complete stranger take control of what *I* used to control. I guess I needed her, but I didn't *want* to need her.

I continued to watch from a distance (metaphorically speaking) because my mind was completely cloudy and mind-drunk from the lack of sugar in my blood cells. Although lying in one place, I felt lost because my thoughts were not flowing or gathering in a comprehensible way. This low-sugar effect was scary, confusing, and nowhere I had ever known myself or my mind to go before. I paid close attention to minuscule objects around me—paperwork, screen displays, beeping sounds—all with no clear lens to where "I" went. I couldn't help but describe it like a video game experience. Little did I realize that this must have been my first hypoglycemic episode.

The nurse kindly handed me two biscuits and a glass of milk. While I didn't realize at the time why I had suddenly become Santa Claus in the wee hours of the morning when everyone else was asleep, I nibbled each bite. Hearing the chomping of my teeth grinding each stale cracker with such intensity, both in force and in volume, my senses had become so amplified. I was quite literally dazed and confused, with all of my other senses on full blast. Hearing, smelling, feeling, seeing—all were working interchangeably to help my body recognize this new phenomenon of survival. This continues to happen, over a decade later, as I place my life on exhibition by sharing the story, that is my life.

Within about twenty minutes, my "blood manager," we'll call her, came to revisit my number. I again sat up and watched this step-by-step process. "You can go back to bed now," she directed me. I looked at her, feeling a bit more Brittany-like, and put my head down. I cried into my pillow, wishing I understood what was happening to me and why I was so deeply disappointed, experiencing such a loss of control. I questioned whether my life would ever be the same. All of these steps, and orders and fears, and beeping, and managing numbers every two hours of my waking day...what was happening to me? I stared at my best friend who lay on the broken sofa the hospital was kind enough to supply. I watched as her feet swung in the air and her spine lay bent in the crease of a been-around-the-block type of couch that's seen too many visitors. Nikki didn't know that I cried while watching her and feeling her love as I suffered. But every day, I am humbled and I appreciate that moment in my life in which I was forced to see something beautiful in a situation that was anything but. My angel was near my side to comfort me, breathe the same air, and hold my hand as we did when we were children, eating apples and watching Nickelodeon. Only now, things were different.

I've learned that through revealing yourself, others will come to see you for who you really are. I am not someone who would just accept a label and the judgments or misconceptions that came with this new lifestyle. I had to learn to see the larger picture—I had to learn to see a gift in my world that seemed so shattered. I had to learn, discover, and become the way I am now, for my own sanity. I wonder if Nikki knows how much I appreciated her being there for me, watching the rising and falling of her chest as she breathed in life and peace, and thinking that it could be mine again, someday, too. It took time, but that odd night, I fell back to sleep and awoke the next day with a realization: every story, including my own, has a beginning, a middle, and an end. Every story will continue—so long as we let it. And no story is worth closing after one disappointing event. I changed the alarm. I was ready to wake up. I learned to read the manual, watch my device (that is, my body), and send an invitation to myself for my next best vision for life.

I was grateful to wake up and eat breakfast that morning: an egg sandwich on whole wheat bread. I was excited for two reasons. One, I had the gift of another day and being alive to experience it. Two, I recognized my Grandpa's birthday was on the day of my diagnosis. I realized that this was *no* coincidence. I knew I had another angel still with me on the day I set out to change my life forever. My body's alarm was set, just as the alarms on my meter that I was learning to use. I walked hand in hand with my new "best friend," my blood sugar meter, whom I would get to know very closely over the course of my life and my journey to find my true purpose.

CHAPTER FIVE

Adjustment ... A "Just Meant"

Leaving the hospital was like a great "SALE" day at Macy's. I walked out with creased clothing and a shiny, "hot" messy hair bun while carrying a whole bunch of bags filled with items I had collected during my stay. I had a schedule that I needed to follow for when I should eat and how many grams of carbohydrate I was allowed. I learned how to calculate the amount of insulin I needed for each time of day, with injections at least five times daily and one high dose of a long-acting insulin at night. Needless to say, this system of learning how to survive using insulin dosing and counting carbs—doing the manual labor of figuring out how many grams of carbohydrate are in each part of my breakfast, lunch, and dinner plate—made eating anything but easy. I used sliding scales, measuring cups, and pen and paper to tally each part of my meal—my dining companions would commonly finish before I could even get started.

With frustration, I would eat foods recommended to me by the nutritionist I met with for several sessions on how to control my diabetes. I carried snack packs, juice boxes and glucose tabs as part of my emergency stash and learned to structure my day with enough time allocated to eat exactly the same amount of carbohydrates, at the exact same time, every day, for *each* meal. Years later, after many quick fix workshops on how to treat hypoglycemia, I recognized that the popular and recommended

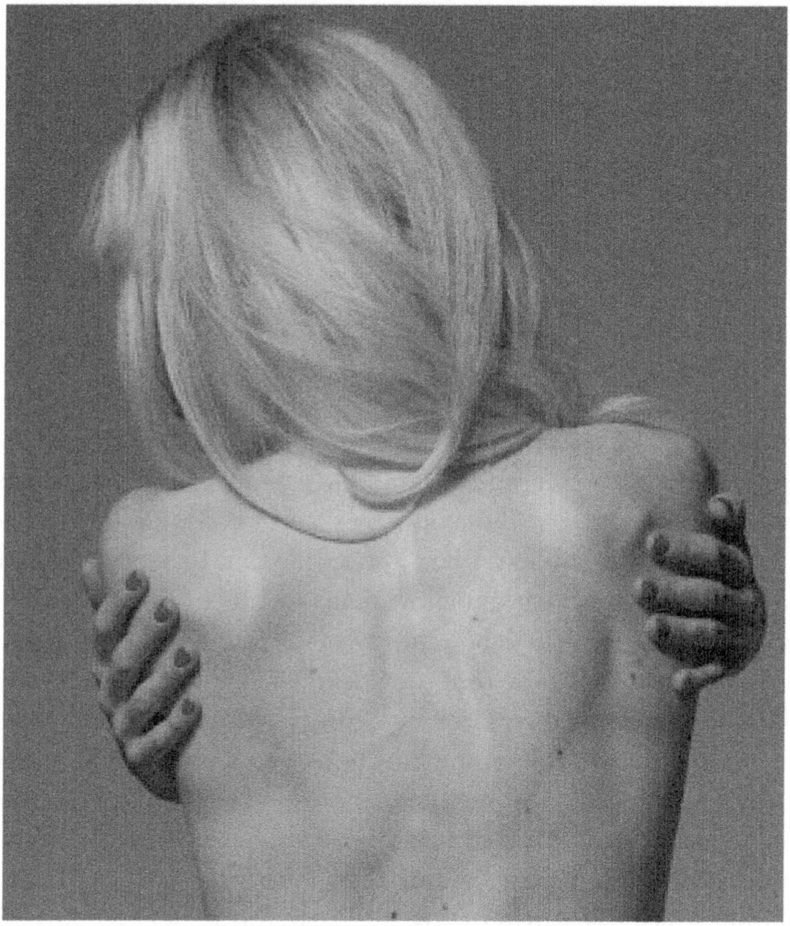

Photographer: Marty Gottlieb

"sugar-free" or "fortified" snack foods that were so frequently recommended would take a toll on *anyone's* overall health, let alone a diabetic's!

To be compliant, I followed the protocol and ate everything with a knife and chisel, if you know what I mean. I tried to practice patience with myself. As food grew cold, and chewing became calculated and slow, I established my set ratio of insulin to carbs and plunged a sharp needle through my belly or thigh when I was finished eating. I would watch my chest quickly rise and fall, oxygen held tightly in my nose, for the pain and instant anxiety I had to cause myself. "Does that hurt?" my friends in the college cafeteria would ask. "OHHH, no, no! This needle? The six-millimeter dagger? No way...this beauty was designed with such precision that it glides right through the tissue and penetrates just like coconut oil on a pan!" I'd say to myself. "And it's so comforting to pinch my fat in public to conceal myself so everyone around me doesn't ask me questions about whether or not I'm shooting up!" I'd mumble. (Yes, I've gotten that, too.) No wonder I felt so lost and upset when I got home the first few days, weeks, and months; I was, as my medical ID would proclaim, "INSULIN-DEPENDENT." I had the bruises and calloused fingertips to prove it.

All these objects, IDs, alerts, conversations with lengthy explanations, and education...was there a reason for this? I couldn't help but be angry—resentful—questioning why I was now different and separate from everyone else. I am fully aware that the mind has the ability to understand things that the human eye can't perceive, so I stayed quiet, prayed, and asked for forgiveness for whatever I had done to deserve this. Often—even in regard to the reasons behind my writing this book—I have thought about how guilt is a prime factor in our assessment of why things do or do not happen in our favor.

What I needed to recognize is that a source or power had this event in my life happen, not as a setback but as a Divine stepping-stone to accept responsibility and reclaim my life. But, it would take time, patience and discipline to develop and understand. Did you know that this same power and opportunity is within you, too? If you can believe that life is a journey during which you can create the life you desire, despite the events that do or do not take place on your own timetable, inner peace and harmony can be achieved! How does it make you feel to know that just by making one simple choice, one life-altering decision, you can create and can have the happiness you've always dreamed of?

Believe that certain things in life are not to be seen as negative, or require an "adjustment," but just as, shall we say, a moment. *Yeah*...I think I like that better. A moment is all we need to reset ourselves to the values we hold for ourselves and our lives. In a moment, we can decide we are meant for so much more...this little fork in the road? It was just a moment—one that struck my heart with light and allowed me to wake up and shout "Brittany's got her groove back!"

CHAPTER SIX

LEARNING THE ABC's OF MY A1C...

Three months into welcoming my new lifestyle, I struggled with a desire to hide myself from the world. I ate in private locations, such as bathroom stalls, to avoid judgment and questions. I also tried to hide my body by purchasing more loose, flowing tunic tops than I could afford. When it was finally time for my check-up, I went to an endocrinologist recommended to me by my mother, who had heard fantastic things about his expertise. His name was Dr. Barry Schuval, an incredible soul whom I would come to know very well over the course of my life.

Later, I would realize the impact this one person has had on my ability to feel optimistic and comforted by this disease. (I always hated that word, because when you break it apart, it's dis-ease. This is the correlation between your mind and body being at rest—when it's not, you are likely to see uncomfortable effects.) Upon recognizing this, I had acknowledged that I never really did feel comfortable in my own skin. Diabetes was just something else that made me feel like I wanted to sink into a hole. That is, until I met my endocrinologist and started on the proper care. It kinda felt like signing up for a subscription to an online dating site, only in this pairing, it was to find a reputable doctor as a lifelong partner in my health. Luckily, I hit the nail on the head the first time around and found the sweetest, smartest, most dedicated, suitable doctor I would ever meet. I guess you could say we were a match from the get-go.

As I walked into the chilly air-conditioned waiting room packed with coughing, belching, deer-in-the-headlights, seasoned people, I found myself seeking individuals who projected what I felt I once had—youthfulness, joy, confidence. I played visions in my head of someone magically pulling out an insulin pen and feeling an immediate relief that I was not alone, running across the room, and hugging them like this diagnosis never happened. Of course, my daydreams seemed silly...but my mind showed me how vulnerable I had become. I sought a sense of optimism or goal achieving...hope that everything would be okay. Unfortunately, that didn't happen. I was the youngest in the room, surrounded by people who seemed to harp on the ills, the pain, the disappointment. Still, I knew our goals were the same: to feel well. I sat with my mom, waiting to meet the professional man who would be seeing me *every* three months for management of my blood sugars.

"Brittany Hines?" a woman with a loud, inviting voice called out over the noise. I stood up and walked down the winding hallways, passing patient rooms full of butcher paper tables, tons of folders, and racing nurses with blood vials to my right. I felt my heart racing. "I'm just going to take your blood sugar," the nurse said.

"Okay" I affirmed as I looked the other way. "OUCH!!!!!" I exclaimed (as I usually would).

Nothing hurts more than having a needle unexpectedly penetrate your skin with unpredicted force. Maybe this is the magic God gives to us warrior diabetics: at some point, when you do it yourself, it becomes second nature, like grabbing a bite of popcorn out of a bag! Desensitized? Maybe. Or maybe, it's just The One being entirely present and allowing room for acceptance, vulnerability, strength, and being mindful of time and matter.

"Now, I'm just going to check your blood pressure. Your weight. Your height. Your oxygen level. And if you could then just pee in this cup for me and bring it back to me with your name on it when you're done. Then, we'll go over your current carb ratios and dosing rates."

I smiled. Half of the smile was because of her kindness in helping me and being soft-natured while doing her job. The other half was my fear, my worry—"I don't *want* to do this!" "Who are you and why is this happening?"—and my "I CAN DO IT MYSELF! LEAVE ME ALONE!" attitude.

Midway through my sharing of what felt like a stock exchange report of information on my current every-two-hour meal bolusing (dosing, for those who know not the diabetes lingo) and correlating blood stick numbers, a medium-statured man entered the room wearing the imagined white lab coat and a beamy smile. It was Dr. Barry Schuval. He slid to the edge of the desk and, before rushing to do panels and interrogate me, gently put his clipboard aside.

"Hi, Brittany! How are you feeling today? It's so wonderful to meet you!"

Captured by his friendly demeanor and sensitive bedside manner, I answered him calmly, yet hesitantly. I felt comfortable just being in his presence. Unlike some doctors I had experienced, he took his time. He asked me questions about my likes, my dislikes, what I did for work, my upbringing and history. But the thing I loved most was that he genuinely showed he cared. He listened—he didn't brush me off to get to the next person with a "problem." It was apparent that I wasn't an item on a to-do list to him.

As my mom and I explained the odd symptoms I'd had during the week or two before my diagnosis—the absurd amount of belching; the urgency to drive home, speeding, just to get food *immediately* after class; the excessive hunger and thirst—Dr. Schuval nodded his head and took notes, treating me as someone he truly wanted to get to know and help. He explained that he would do some blood work and call me in about three days to discuss the results. I felt secure and in Spirit-like hands. About forty minutes after getting to meet him and talk about Diabetes 101 treatment, I gave him a wide, open wave goodbye like I was holding a flag at Disneyworld. Looking back, all the signs and energy from above were telling me: *I will be OK. I am safe here.* I watched him carefully close the door behind him as the nurse re-entered the room.

I chose to display a toothy smile as, embarrassed, I went to the bathroom with my empty cup and returned with a fully loaded one, as if it held all the answers to my queries. Then, I could, you know, get back to my life. The nurse smiled back and wrapped my arm with a tight rubber band to make my veins "juicy." (Ew!) "Just, if you could pump your fist for me," she asked. There were a couple of things that I would have liked to have pumped my fist for. But I did as she asked, inhaling and exhaling deeply, hearing the whizzing of my blood pouring into several vials with my name on them. I prayed, and I watched, as if I were watching my life from somewhere else. It felt like I was watching myself from a separate body or from a separate lens—*"weird,"* I thought. I imagined myself outside of this situation and sat with a glazed look, analyzing every moment. My mind wandered and then wandered some more. I stayed motionless, but I felt a piece of peace, knowing that I had found the right match, one that would help me to feel whole again.

CHAPTER SEVEN

You're Hired! I Mean, Fired!

The feelings I had, living daily life with diabetes, fluctuated like the weather. Some days, I felt happy and "in range," but other times I cried—nauseous, unable to eat, and urinating out the sugar my body wasn't able to process. I came to understand what both "high" sugar felt like and what "low" sugar felt like. My blood sugar readings over 150 left me feeling dazed and confused, irritable, unable to concentrate, and with frequent trips to the bathroom. My low blood sugar readings left me feeling scattered with heart palpitations, sweatiness, utter confusion, a sweetness to my tongue, and total brain fog.

I guess you could say I slowly learned to navigate my new life with my diabetic "updates." I got pretty good at timekeeping: I knew when it was time to eat and when I needed to give myself more insulin. I learned to listen to my body's call for attention to flow with the rhythm of daily living. On "good days" I tried to tackle the world, accomplishing all that I could. Subconsciously, I tried to make up for the things I couldn't do on the days my sugar was not in my target range, and needing rest, despite my best efforts to have it do what I *wanted* it to do. On one of these strong moments, I took advantage of the energetic feeling and picked up a side waitressing gig to help me make some extra money to support myself.

With my goal in mind, I sallied forth to a popular American restaurant nearby. Within moments of my cheery self entering to fill out an application, I was hired on the spot! "Yay!" I thought, and immediately began studying the menu, drinks, and specials to prepare for my first official day. Knowing how seriously I took myself and my work, I was confident that I could make enough money to be useful in helping to support my active lifestyle and my mission to cure myself by getting whatever I needed—whether it be a stem-cell procedure that had been known to "cure" Type 1 patients, a fridge full of organic food, or just a vacation to get away from myself. I later learned that I never could get away from myself, so I'd better start loving myself, *now!*

As a classy, feminine lady wearing a collared white button-down, black tie, businessman-like trousers, and enough hair gel to slick every bit of my "Goldilocks" hair away from my face, I must've been *incredibly* motivated. Subconsciously, I think I was hoping to make enough money to help me escape from my body and my current circumstances. Keeping diabetes my secret, I signed up for double shifts, sometimes forgetting to eat and ignoring the fact that my blood sugars were dropping due to all the walking from table to table, from early morning to past midnight.

I found a way to get by: swigging a Coca-Cola behind the computer system, finding comfort in the fact that, like me, everyone else there was just trying to stay afloat in a beyond-busy atmosphere. Luckily, I found a secure space where I could keep my lunch bag packed with "safe" food in case there was a lull between lunch and dinner and I could satisfy my need to eat.

One particular evening, my manager, Mindy, was yelling for us waitstaff to "Get on the floor...full hands, full hands! Move it! We have a forty-five-minute wait; I don't want to see anyone slacking here right now—I said, *GET ON IT*!" Feeling the sweatiness of my palms and confused about which direction to go to get to table 9, my world began to seem like a video game—a feeling I'd had many times before. Out of fear, I pushed myself to keep walking, keep moving, and grab all the hot plates I could hold with my long "piano fingers" as my childhood teacher would always call them. I held two steak plates in one arm and a Caesar salad with dressing in the other.

By the time I rushed to serve the waiting guests, I couldn't stop my mind and body from shutting down. My fingers lost their grip on the salad dressing and I watched it topple to the floor. The other hand slowly lost control, too, as I watched the french fries spill onto the gentleman's lap. Mindy looked at me with tight, pursed lips and disapproval. I felt like a failure. I knew I was in trouble. "Here we go. I'm about to get scolded for not doing what I was *supposed* to do," I thought. I went to the back of the kitchen to find my lunchbox with my emergency food items. "Where is my lunchbox?" I thought, wiping tears from my eyes. I looked...and looked...and looked. "Did someone eat my glucose tabs and my snacks? Why would someone take my insulin from my coolpack? That wouldn't be very professional, let alone, humanlike—who would *do* that?" I asked myself. I began circulating around the kitchen asking the chefs and the waitstaff if they had seen my lunchbox. "Nope. Haven't seen it. Sorry," said the men. "I *did* see it, but I don't know where it went," said another employee, Jessie. "Maybe you forgot it at home. I've never seen it before," said another.

I became angry, frustrated, upset, and hurt. Two double whammies in one night—I *hated* this feeling. Determined to find my bag, I mustered up the courage to ask Mindy to make an announcement about my emergency-food stash gone missing. She looked at me, not understanding the importance, and said she would review the videos from the kitchen. It turned out someone *did* throw my lunch bag away in the garbage. I guess they thought I was just hungry and keeping snacks for myself. I guess they thought it wouldn't be a big deal...but, it *was*.

The evening ended with a discussion about the importance of "professionalism" with my manager. I felt my heart pounding and knew from her tone that no matter what I said about my diabetes, she wouldn't understand. I needed to get the job done and she didn't care how I did it. Driving home, I ripped off my ugly black tie, pulled out my tight bun and the horrible hair pins that got stuck in my hair, and blasted my music wanting to just *get away*!

I fell asleep that night knowing I had to be strong enough to return the next day, because I couldn't be a quitter. That's not who I am. I *needed* to be strong. I *needed* to prove that I could work, and work well—that I *was* like everyone else. I made it my mission to not only do what everyone else could do, but also to learn to do it *better.* As morning approached, I affirmed to myself that today would be a new day. I would forget about the hurtful events of the night before and stick to my plan.

Pushing the heavy steel doors open to begin my shift, I got the news.

"Brittany, can you come speak with me for a minute?" asked Mindy.

"Sure, not a problem!" I replied.

"So, me and the other manager have been talking, and, although we think you're a *really* sweet girl, and you *really* did well with our clientele and selling all the specials, we feel like you would be better off somewhere else. We feel like you're fragile. We want you to be happy doing something that you enjoy and that you like to do."

"What? But, I am happy here. I do like it here," I tried to explain.

"We just think it will be better for us and for you if you move on. You're just...fragile, you know?"

I *didn't* know. I didn't want to accept that. I fought the tears, knowing I was being discriminated against because of my disability. Never wanting to cause an issue or concern, and trusting that Universe is always working for my highest good, I walked away. I left my thoughts unspoken. With my head down but my mind ever strong, I thought about how I would prove them wrong. I thought about what I could do to become who I needed to be. With that, I peaced out, and made the best decision that I had ever made in my life: it was time for me to get in control of my diabetes and take care of myself. I would go on an insulin pump! Fragile? Let me show you just *how* strong I am.

CHAPTER EIGHT

A Jane Fonda Kinda Toot

One quote that I often think of is this one from the Greek philosopher Heraclitus: "The only constant in life is change." Remembering and welcoming this philosophy into my life, I've learned to trust and know, in my most pure heart, that everything is and will be okay. In fact, life will be *more* than okay, even though all of the answers are not spelled out right here, right now. I've learned that change can be a great thing because it helps us to detach ourselves from our "stuck" ways of being. Going with the flow, and being in the dance of life, allows all that is meant to be, to be...in perfect time, space, and sequence.

Looking for a connection with my inner self to rise and emerge, I began spending more time each day doing things that lifted my spirit. I spent time brainstorming and identifying the things that made me smile and laugh. I remembered that one of my passions has always been music! Mom said that when I was a baby, I could be all by my lonesome and bopping my head to a catchy beat, with not a care in the world. Well, after living my life with Type 1 diabetes and wanting to tap into and bring alive the happiness that had been lost, I sought activities that would bring back that bee-boppin' *spirit* within me. I found myself eager to sign up and go to Zumba classes left and right, so I made this a part of my regular routine. I refused to judge myself for not knowing the correct salsa spins or lyrics. Rather, I invited myself to the *opportunity* of feeling as part of a community of others who also loved to wiggle, drop, bounce and forget the stresses of the outside world for a while, too. Simultaneously, I pursued other personal desires, such as striving to achieve optimal health through mind and body exercises like weight training, yoga, Pilates, and meditation. This was my updated form of feeling and expressing happiness in my current stage and age.

One particular summer evening, the sun shone on my face as I drove to my nightly step aerobics class at the local gym. I sang with the windows down as I made my way through rush hour traffic, anticipating the songs and the feelings they would bring forth that night. Doesn't everyone just love to live loosely, freely, and happily? That was me! Like Gumby, no matter how much tugging, dropping, or pulling, I learned the importance of stretching myself, mentally and physically, to *always* remain resilient.

When I arrived in class, I put my belongings down and checked my blood sugar before bringing my more confident self to the mirror. I left my rice cakes, juice, sugar tabs, and Glucagon emergency kit to the side while I hiked up my tank top. The music began thumping and the instructor, Pamela, began coaching the class in the moves we would be doing. As I began to stop, drop, and pop it, I began to feel my elevated blood sugars slowly melt away. One arrow popped up on my device. "OK," I thought, "Let me just keep an eye on where this is going."

I felt the vibration of my medical device buzz against my hip and I knew it was time to address the low blood sugar reading that was coming on. As I pressed the buttons on my medical device to stop the vibration, I heard a roar over the upbeat music. *"PUT THE CELL PHONE AWAY!"* Pamela shouted over the microphone.

"Wait a minute," I thought, "Is she talking to me?" I looked up as the short-haired blonde approached me with a pitbull-ish look to reprimand me on her 80's looking head speaker set for all the class to hear. I was *mortified*! As I lost my focus out of humiliation and complete astonishment, the 32-inch cord of my insulin pump swung back and forth with the springiness of a Zipline bungee rope. As she scolded me, I raised my eyes from the ground to meet hers. I apologized and found myself, once again, explaining who I was and what I have. My voice rose to top the intensity of the music, fighting for control. I knew I was more than *this*.

"I have Type 1 diabetes. This is my medical device! I need it to live; it was beeping and needed my attention," I tried to explain.

Pamela's face dropped as she bit her lip and wiped sweat beads from her forehead, obviously regretting her aggressiveness. "Oh! My cat is diabetic. I give her shots..."

I couldn't help but look at her with disgust as my life was broadcast on the room's speakers for everyone to hear. I almost forgot that my favorite song was playing in the background—I had checked out and had lost my sense of fun. I tried to remind myself of my goal: to rise above my circumstances and live up to my fullest potential! I knew in my heart I couldn't stop—there was more to my story, that is my life. I got back up and thought about my dream to create positive change for those living like myself, with a diagnosis or setback, leaving a lasting impact on those who may *never* understand. I lifted my foot and began stepping and dancing to the beat of my own drum, again.

CHAPTER NINE

The Intentional Interview

Well-known spiritual teacher Deepak Chopra once said, "In the midst of movement and chaos, keep stillness inside you." A simple notion, with such density, it allows for the whispers of wisdom to be granted entry into the mind. In my early adult years, this was what I would grow to appreciate as I tried to find myself and the truth of my existence. I sought to finally seek that which I had previously been too busy to see—from what or from whom I was hiding from.

I struggled to answer this question for quite a while, as many of us do. I'm sure if you are reading this book, you may have felt the same way. It's that feeling of being home and wanting to be out, but when we're out, wanting to be home. Sounds confusing, right? Let alone understanding other people! At times, it can seem we don't even understand...*ourselves*. For those who let it, life will continue as a persistent state of discomfort with where and who we are...unless we *ask* the questions we need to ask ourselves and *sit* with our emotions and our feelings long enough to understand them. This is how we can receive our own answers. To eradicate this feeling, we must start digging to try to know ourselves more intrinsically.

Often, it's not the answers that we find, but the questions, that lead to a deeper understanding of the self. After countless attempts to isolate myself because of my belief that I was separate or unworthy, I realized that I was creating this void *myself*. I later recognized that some of the answers were not meant for me to find. Maybe the purpose of life *is* to have passion and desire to understand *ourselves* before we can understand the people, experiences, and lessons in this world.

No matter the age, the place, or the circumstances, I've learned that the questions will always come, always flow, and always form and reform themselves. Are our lives and our life purpose not one big mystery? Our human nature itself may sometimes be quite demanding, expecting answers on our own timetable, though we do not know how long we will be *here*. Our lives may become more meaningful if a shift is made: to be at peace with the asking of our questions and trust that at the right time, in the right place, and in exactly the right sequence, the answers *will* be revealed. It may serve us to look at the deeper root, which is the formation of the question, and *why* it has surfaced or continues to resurface. This type of behavior would not only help us assess our current state of mind, but our subconscious beliefs about ourselves that we may not yet be fully aware of, if at all.

I have faith that there is a higher force, a Greater Power, above all creation that is responsible for the beauty, life force, lessons, and blessings we each are intended to experience in this life. The power that I hold to be God may also be widely recognized as Universe, Spirit, Almighty, Light, or the Divine. These terms are used interchangeably in my writing; they all express the belief that there is something real that is bigger than you or I could ever possibly conceive of—The One Almighty Presence. Surrounding and filling us always, this Divine energy is in and around every part of existence. Like Einstein's scientific understandings have led us to believe, energy "can neither be created nor destroyed." It is ever-changing, ever-existing, ever-evolving, as is our world and our unique works within it.

My faith, though it has been a continuous journey that gives me greater clarity and fulfillment, has gone through periods when I have cried out, feeling helpless. Especially, when I knew I was spreading myself too thin and subconsciously ignoring the need to manage my stress and take care of myself and my diabetes.

A part of me *knew* what I needed to do: eat with intention to nourish and heal my body, and keep my body moving through exercise. But sometimes I didn't want to feel like I was taking care of myself on a schedule.

It seemed selfish of me to make time for myself. Let alone time to maintain an active social life with dating and friends. Still, I knew that taking care of myself was absolutely essential to my new desire of changing old patterns and living a "whole" life. I needed to leave behind the old thoughts and old memories that tried to keep me where I was. I knew by doing this, I could nurture my soul back to health, one day at a time.

Feeling pressured to meet the demands of others' expectations, I retreated to the comfortable layers of blankets on my bed, drawing the blinds shut, and struggling with leaving behind my already established pattern of living in safety mode, away from everyone and everything. I found parts of myself still trying to hold onto the past, still trying to satisfy who my boss, my colleagues, my ego, and weirdly enough, who my unlovable self wanted me to be. I struggled with living and speaking my truth. I felt out of alignment or more frequently termed, "out of control" because of the way I internalized and responded to *other* people's thoughts and expectations. I had subconsciously made them my own. While I did my best *at* work, I hadn't even begun the *self*-work my body needed to heal.

Depression ran in my family, but I never wanted to admit that it had lingered in me, especially during the time of my diagnosis. I hid out of fear of being judged and fear of people finding out the "truth" of who was behind the long, flowy blonde hair and bright blue eyes. I felt like I was wearing a mask throughout the day, one that I took off when I got home to reveal the vulnerable, don't-have-it-all-figured-out Britt. I placed huge expectations on myself, and I was never so sure as to why. Each morning, I put on a fresh pretty blouse and a layer of my favorite berry pink lipstick to match my manicured toes. I was covering up a soul that had a deep need for love and some serious self-care. But,But I didn't know how to "fix" the parts of myself that I didn't approve of anymore.

I continued a cyclical pattern of isolating myself, tucking myself away wherever space would lend itself...my car, my bedroom, my classroom, the beach, or my favorite place, my headphones. I found myself arranging social outings in such a way that it became convenient to run away when I felt vulnerable. To friends, my usual response for a coffee meet or light Sunday brunch would be, "Oh don't mind me; I'll meet you there!" Dinner plans? "Ah! Don't worry about me. It's usually hard for me to share appetizers because I can't eat anything fried, or that has sugar. I'll probably just get a plate of vegetables, make it easy..." I would explain. I learned to protect myself, consoling my soul in an invisible tortoise shell each time life handed me the opportunity to stand up and be strong. I guess I just thought by doing so, it would all just...go away.

"You can't even have just a little bit of pasta? We'll share," my girlfriends would insist.

"Well, no, it makes me have brain fog when I eat too many carbohydrates at one sitting; I won't feel right. Plus, they usually use tomato sauce and butter, which has a later effect..." I stopped myself there. I couldn't stand to hear myself talk about the things I couldn't have. I couldn't stand to feel pity. I didn't want it. I felt like it was just easier for me to keep it all inside...plus, I knew they wouldn't understand the trial-and-error experiments that I've conducted on myself over the years. I would just seem like a paranoid organic and Whole Foods–only chick.

As I sat there wallowing in doubt and shame with questions as to why my life had become so different from theirs, I still felt this urge to educate them so they could understand what just a day in my life was like. Maybe it was just so I could feel accepted. I felt unworthy, and my spirit reflected that.

When I was reminded of my love for writing, I began to keep a journal in an attempt to get to know myself and become my own best friend, again. My ideas, thoughts, and feelings were naturally translated into words page after page. I started to see light through the shadows I had created, that really never existed, after all. My spirit felt comfortable and at peace, basking in the light, feeling a sense of utter freedom.

Writing has always been my source of joy and liberation. It was my cozy spot, where I let my hands say what my spoken words seemed to withhold. I allowed myself to embrace this passion, continuing to rewrite my own story and become the free soul I had known myself to be. I knew that I wanted to hold onto this light...and *be* this light.

Finding my secret joy allowed me to write the book of myself, in which I could acknowledge where I was, where I am now, and where I would like to be. The choice and the responsibility were up to *me*. I know your secret joy is within *you,* too! Just waiting to be discovered, loved, appreciated, recognized, and validated.

- What does *joy* look like for you?
- What does it *sound* like?
- What are you *doing* when you feel it?

Dream about the hobbies, interests, and passions you used to have, and think about the time you spent doing them. Once you have come up with what I like to call a "Bliss List," spend time developing yourself with these secret life-enhancers that bring you back to that place of happiness and love. Make time to become present in your *own* life experience, because *you* matter. Not because of what you have or have not done, but because you *exist*.

CHAPTER TEN

Compatibility with Self and Others

Have you ever wished that you understood yourself, your choices, and the patterns in your life with more clarity? I know I have. Often, I've found myself analyzing, replaying, and attempting to relive past events while anticipating future ones. I couldn't help but notice that much of my focus had left the present moment—the most *important* moment! The only moment that *really* matters...the *now!* This is where meditation has really helped me, especially, as I have been living my life with a new vision. Sometimes the most powerful messages come through in absolute and utter silence. Just self, mind, and God.

As I continue to gather my recollections of my growth since my diagnosis, I recall all the experiences I have had—*yes,* even the hardships—and I wonder *how* exactly I got here. By reviewing my life, looking back at these moments in time, I am guided to understand and recognize that there was not just one conversation or one *aha!* moment, but rather a series of life experiences that have helped shape and form my respective beliefs, goals and values. It's just kind of that *tapping-into-yourself* thing that occurs when we are put in situations that challenge us to be in stillness, accept what is, and surrender to the now. By reviewing my life, and looking back at these moments in time,

I felt guided to understand and make sense of my patterns, subconscious beliefs, and thoughts.

This revisitation to the parts of my life that have had such an impact on me are the life experiences that have helped mold my current values, goals, and beliefs that I am living out. I recognize the times in my life when I *thought* I was forced to feel upset, hurt, or disappointment. I recognize *today* that spending endless time reliving an event serves no purpose to moving into the bountiful future that is in the hands of each and every one of us. It is the *present* moment that invites us to experience the rich fullness of our very being and our astonishingly beautiful essence of being truly alive.

I like to think of the human body and experience as a gift. Even though I have been tested, believe me: "Oh! You got diabetes because you ate too much sugar." "Can you take off your machinery?" "What *is* that? Are you going to be on that for the rest of your life?" "That sucks...chocolate is *so* good! I feel bad you can't enjoy what we all can." These comments are all so hurtful when I think of them. I can't help what other people say, do, or feel. But, I *could*, however; change the way that I let these statements affect me. I *could*...release them. I *could* change how I look at my life *and* how I live it. I had a choice to change how I viewed my *own* worth and my very *own* image. Now, I've understood the value of choosing to surround myself with people who love and support the woman that I *am*. Not the woman I once was, or the woman I could or should be.

I've learned that we often can learn from our conversations—with ourselves and others. I'll give you an example. I once dated a guy whom I fell head over heels for, as quickly as you can say "hot potato." I was *in*. He was charming and good looking, and it seemed like he had it all together (he did a great job of dressing the part and creating that illusion). We'll call this person "Joey." Joey was one of my subconscious "attachments." In the teachings of Buddha, attachments are explained as our cravings—what we want more and more of, and it's complete opposition, what we actually want less of. This constant cycle of wanting versus not wanting leaves human beings in a constant cycle of desire. In simple terms, I tend to think of an attachment as anything or anyone that occupies more space in your mind than considered normal and can cause feelings of obsessing or idolizing.

If you're not so sure what a healthy mind thinks like, here is an example: If you find yourself continuously fixed on *someone* or *something*, and you are giving most of your awake attention to *them* or *it*...then you have subconsciously checked out of *yourself*—therefore; this is an attachment. Attachments can bring us back to that familiar, judgmental part of ourselves where it becomes easier to latch onto someone or something than to actually look at ourselves. We do this in hopes that these people or things will fulfill *our need* to be happy. It is sometimes easier for us to put our time and effort into someone or something that we perceive as "better" than us than actually looking at ourselves. These people and things are in fact, no better than us, at all—as we are all *one.* It is a form of not only distraction, but illusion.

Joey was a person who I clung to, mentally, dreaming of the illusion of who he was. He was so charming that he helped me forget about all the other things that *weren't* working in my life. He showered me with affection, time, and spontaneity, and I *loved* it. A diamond necklace and a couple of "I love yous" later, Joey's time in my life had expired. After months of flirting, giggles, and unique dates, as Universe would have it, it was time for an update. When the phone rang this particular day and I saw Joey's name pop up, I sensed something was up, immediately. When I answered, instead of our typical flirtation and giggles, the conversation quickly went to "I just...wish we were more compatible." I was stunned...but, was I really? My senses told me before anything even happened. This was just the way that Universe confirmed what I already felt and knew inside. I share this story as an example of how attachments can sometimes awaken us so that we can know and understand our true self calling.

As I listened to this Joey-guy, for whom I had once had feelings for, say to me that we were not compatible, I searched for clarification. "Why not? We had great chemistry and a connection, you said before..." It took every ounce of acceptance in my soul to listen with an open mind. My intuition was *literally* telling me to let go and move onward, but I found it challenging to simply release. I didn't want to feel rejected—I didn't want to *not* have the last word. I sat quietly, listening to what was being dished out and tried to understand, despite being uncomfortable.

Joey gave me a direct, albeit shaky, response. "Well, sometimes I wish we could do things together. Like I could go out to eat with you and order a steak with potatoes or choose a restaurant and not have to question where I'm bringing you because of what you can and cannot have," he apprised. I gulped as if he had punched me in the chest. "Ouch," I thought. He continued, as though what he had already said wasn't hurtful enough. "Like, if I wanna go somewhere, I don't wanna have to think, 'Oh, she can't eat that, we can't go there.' I want to be with someone who—we can share things, and we like the same things. I don't know. It takes a strong person to date someone who eats and has to live as you do." I couldn't believe what I was hearing! And I had *feelings* for this dude? Too young to recognize and appreciate whom I was giving my heart to, I couldn't fathom the heartlessness of these comments. I mean, didn't he *understand* that it's not by choice that I got diabetes? Still, I couldn't help but wonder if I was sending off signals that I wasn't even conscious of.

As I watched myself swish papers across the kitchen table, trip over my sneakers, push chairs in that were askew, I recognized and experienced my frustration. I was angry, I was upset, I was at a loss for words...and...*there* it came! One of those old feelings, rehashed from previous years, zipped through my inner stream. One thought after the next began to race through my mind—"I'm not good enough. I'm not worthy enough. I'm not lovable. I'm different." My ego tried to get a hold of me...and unknowingly, I gave in. I sat on the other end of the phone line, thinking, as I heard him explain that he knew he was "making the right choice."

I couldn't help but interject and stand up for myself and for every single person living with a condition for which they are wrongly and selfishly judged by others. I felt that passion in my heart (the same passion that compelled me to write this book) and mustered something to say that would kindly, but surely, shut this person's ability to hurt me *down*.

"Well, you know what? I'm sorry you feel that way. I like to keep my body and my mind in tip-top shape—that's a priority for me. And also, I agree! We are *not* compatible. Because although we had our differences and there may be some things about you that I don't understand, I don't seek to change you or remake you in my image. I love who I am. I'm happy with the way I live my life. And for the record, I'd like to date someone where we appreciate and value each other. Build experiences and love. For me, it's about the connection—not the food."

Still replaying the conversation in my mind, it was important for me to remind myself of my *own* worth and remain optimistic that these relationships with other people—friends, family, neighbors, lovers, strangers, healers, colleagues—are all placed in our lives for a reason. These relationships serve as a mirror of ourselves—to teach, trigger growth, or help us or another in some way, whether it is easily recognizable or not. These staple relationships and connections serve as representations of *ourselves* to examine. We attract what *we* believe.

I felt proud of myself, for once, for finally standing up for *myself*. Standing up for my life and my values and for discovering my purpose. I had finally chosen to forego the illusion of finding happiness in other people and things for which it could never be found. The reality I had come to know was that *I* am responsible for creating my own happiness. It would all start with releasing, forgiving, and loving myself, *first!* I chose to let go of the *illusion* that I wasn't worthy of love, because this time around, I *knew* that I was, and I know that I always *am*. There is no room for hatred or judgment in my path, anymore. Now, I know that I was created *exactly* the way I was meant to be. Every experience I have had has molded me into the woman I was created to be: a woman who is living her strongest, happiest, and most fulfilling life, on purpose. I'm better than I was, I'm stronger because of what I've been through, and I am *grateful* because there is a whole lifetime ahead of me to celebrate this truth! I've learned through this journey and in discovering my strength, that I *matter.* Brittany *matters*.

I've grown to believe through my experience that God doesn't give me, or anyone, *anything* they can't handle. I trust that I am being used as an instrument to help develop the Divine plan that Universe has *already* set for me. When I say I wholeheartedly, willingly, and openly believe this—I *believe* it. Now, it's time for *you* to do some self-work!

- How do you mirror your own beliefs in your own life?
- Who or what drives the vehicle of your soul?
- Is it your mind? Your heart? Your voice? Or perhaps, is it others?
- What would it take to recognize the entirety of the complete person you already are?
- How might this vision shift to become all that you dream of your life to be?

Take time to dream...envision...create...and LIVE—because you can do it, too.

CHAPTER ELEVEN

Purchasing My Own One-Way Ticket

I once had a conversation that would have a tremendous impact on who I was—and who I had chosen to become. Although I was quite shy and earned names like Lamb and The Wallflower, my inner self was always present, inside me...somewhere. I got to know the voice inside myself, with whom I spoke so often with, just by watching, paying close attention to the actions that came naturally, and listening carefully. I mentally recorded things, managed the files in my head, and quietly collected data that would later serve me well in identifying my purpose.

One evening after school, my friends Jennifer and Michelle and I had been kindly "Uber-ed" by one of the parentals to a dance class. A silky rich chocolate Godiva ice cream pint was being circulated around the navy Toyota Rav4 as if auto ice cream parties were what people did. No potato chips for this crew, but instead spoons, napkins, and sloppy chocolate fingers! The mother behind the wheel noticed my discipline and self-control, unusual for one so young.

"Brittany, you don't eat ice cream?" Mrs. Rabino asked.

"Oh, I do; only sometimes, though. I like to eat healthy, so I try to avoid sugar as much as I can," I replied.

"Wow, what will power!" the proud mom exclaimed, as if deeply impressed that someone would *want* to avoid sweets with such diligence and pride.

I stared out the window and took in every thump of the song "The Sign" by Ace of Base while dancing on the inside, smiling, and going my way. What I recognize today is that even then, parents, friends, and other people I came into contact with noticed something unique about me—my true self, though I never identified with the person I was on the inside. I barely noticed each "You're amazing!" or "You're so admirable!" uplifting comment and continued through the years unknowingly collecting and compiling the negative statements instead.

It was as though my ego enjoyed collecting doubtful or limiting statements rather than the celebratory ones. The former seemed to occupy a high-rent area inside my head and be more influential than any other emotional property. I was paying high taxes on myself, so to speak. Although I hated feeling that way, I couldn't seem to convince myself not to. I didn't know how; it seemed hard, if not completely impossible. "How could I change this voice inside my head? It was me, wasn't it?" I thought. Too accustomed to ignoring each thoughtful attempt to do so, I persisted with what had become comfortable rather than helpful.

I listened to others verbalized thoughts and watched and observed the correlating actions *in response* to my own words and actions. I guess subconsciously, I thought I could rely on others telling me more about *me* since they could see me in action. I supposed it was that I didn't trust myself, enough, to be my own best judge of my own self. I listened to the words of everyone around me that were just...said, because they could. Welcomed or not welcomed, the words that I had heard had become my expectations of myself, what I lived up to. It was who I presented myself to the world as, then. You think I'm shy? I am. You think I'm funny? Okay, I can be that. You think I'm too white? Okay. I'll wear more bronzer. This collage of who I was living up to was becoming nothing more than snippets of ripped construction paper pasted on a false, fabricated version of the person *I* knew myself as and that I was *intended* to be. It took days, months, and years to master my own practice— to become mindful, confident, and involved in designing the strong woman I am today.

To what extent have you unknowingly given your power away in your own life? Often, we take on the attitude, personality, or vibration of those we interact with. So, be mindful of who you give your full self to—because you may end up ordering a part of yourself that you'll want to send back to the kitchen, eventually. But, not to worry! Awareness is the first step to ditching the old parts of ourselves that serve us no well. This is when we each have the ability to step in and re-create the vision we have for ourselves and our lives.

CHAPTER TWELVE

THE SOUL OF MY FEET

When I had first begun my teaching career, I learned how special little humans and their thoughts are. Let me explain. There once was a little five-year-old boy whom I had the pleasure of getting to know in the kindergarten class I taught in my second year of teaching. Joshua was a cheerful little boy who came from a big family in which there were more bodies than rooms to sleep in; he had many brothers and sisters. His family taught him the value of having a kind heart and believing in a loving God. I know this because although he had yet to understand phonemes and suffix endings, his beginning stages of writing and illustrations suggested that he had great admiration for and knowledge of this Higher Power.

Although Joshua was not the highest-performing student with the most impressive test scores, I found myself always selecting his work to showcase on fancy bulletin boards because I saw the gifts *inside* him. All year around, I praised Joshua for his diligence and his open soul that was full of love and life to everyone in our classroom community, hoping more students would emulate his type of character. Secretly, it was also because he showed *me* a little bit of the hope that I needed to be reminded of every day.

One morning, as I shuffled from our daily reading lesson into writing, I modeled how to create a narrative writing piece, focusing on something that was important to me. My young little learners had become familiar with all of the clicks and beeps of my medical device as the year progressed. They *knew* what it meant when "Ms. Hines needs two minutes to take care of herself." As I was just about to pop the cap off of my dry erase marker and begin teaching, there it was: the *feeling*. The tingling sensation of my tongue, a rush of adrenaline, confusion, utter panic, sweat, and an indescribable need for glucose.

"Ms. Hines has to go eat now! Everybody quiet" one student shouted. "How did this little three-foot-one-inch child know the protocol?" I thought, as I jumped through the circle of students seated on our plush map-of-the-world rug. I listened as the boys and girls whom I had just moments earlier instructed to gather on the rug revealed themselves as a group of twenty five-year-olds who had learned to understand my condition and behave as sensitive young beings, who had undeniably developed their patience, compassion, and care.

"Ms. Hines has got to eat four of 'em, four of those purple things. Sugar. It's gonna make her feel better," whispered Nyla, a smart and caring young girl with an upbeat disposition and desire to help.

I could have cried at that moment, but I fought it. Without my saying anything, my students were learning that although we are different, we are *still* one. We *all* need love, we *all* need support, and we *all* deserve to be cared for, especially when in need. Sometimes, we just gotta accept our own cry for help and know that it's okay. Little Joshua would later explain this.

Once again, I sat down in my "adult" chair and began to model how to write a narrative. I chose something important to me: my medical ID bracelet. My students had learned why this was an important piece of jewelry for me to wear every day, so I knew it would be the perfect thing to use as my model. I began to write, using the "hamburger strategy," starting with my topic sentence.

"My medical ID bracelet is an important piece of jewelry that represents who I am. "There! My introduction!" I said, "Now, boys and girls, we have to elaborate on this idea so our readers will understand more about me and this special object of mine. Let's continue...'My medical ID is silver and shiny and has my name and information about my health on it. It helps to keep me safe. I love my medical ID bracelet.'"

As I finished my thought and struggled to remain focused to provide closure for my paragraph—at a reading of 40 at finger prick—I found myself biting my lip and mentally trying to perform my role as a teacher like a Broadway star, instantly and magically better within seconds! I think it's a human desire to dream of being in a state of perfection at all times, and especially in front of young kids. As I colored my tomato, lettuce, and juicy brown hamburger patty drawing, I was ready to add the final portion of our paragraph, when all of a sudden, I saw a hand shoot up from the carpet below me. It was Joshua.

"Yes, Joshua? Do you have a question or comment to share?" I asked curiously.

Joshua stared at me, thinking very deeply. He looked me right in the eyes from the front of the circle—I guess you could say where it "started" by my feet—and said to me, gesturing with his tiny hands, "Yeahhhhhh...but, Ms. Hines? God loves you, and"—he looked up toward our ABC chart and poster of shapes—"You're going to be safe because God loves you and He created you. You don't have to worry."

I lost my voice. I lost my train of thought, my direction for the next teaching increment, my sense of trying to control—*everything*. I felt a gentle tear come to my eye as Joshua continued to stare at me. For a moment, I was brought back to the vision that God created for me: that life *is* beautiful, joyful, and free. Every being has the right to feel this. So why is it so easily forgotten and lost? Looking at Joshua's face, along with all of the little listening ears and wiggling bodies, I realized that he had conveyed a message that everyone could appreciate.

I looked up from my sentence on the board and came back to the fullness of life standing right before me and within me. The message was unexpected, but I willingly received it. It was the truth from someone who had not yet lost who he was because of challenging circumstances.

"Thank you, Joshua, thank you," was all that I could slowly and carefully breathe out. "Okay, boys and girls, it's time for you to think about something important to you! Remember the writing structure and try to brainstorm some key details to really pull your reader in!" I exclaimed.

Walking back to my desk, nodding my head in a real *aha!* moment, I reflected on the many little blessings that come through conversations and interactions with others. Maybe, just maybe, it occurred to me, I needed my students as much as they needed me. In that moment, I recognized the *real* power of being present. I appreciated the value of this experience: a moment overcome with love and trust from the voice that comes alive... when you *believe*.

CHAPTER THIRTEEN

Meet Me ... and Subconscious Me

When I became wise enough to know better and desire more than the quality of life I was currently living I started to become more curious about the woman inside of this body. The woman who, though strong in her faith, pursuing a meaningful career, talented, creative, hardworking, and well-educated, defeatedly felt so disconnected from who she was. The physical and emotional parts of myself, and the energy of who I was seemed to be traveling on opposite highways, and I sought direction.

I became reflective about not only the hand I had been dealt but also my life experiences. I recall the time I was pushed to go to soccer camp to have fun while kindly giving Mamadukes and Poppadukes a break over the summer. I remember being bullied into walking around the soccer field with my back hunched over, neighing like a freakin' donkey. Yep...that was me! The little blonde girl, afraid of the world and afraid of speaking up for herself, *was* me.

A decade later, and a diagnosis of Type 1 diabetes under my belt, I became not only inquisitive about how to heal myself but incredibly determined to leave what *used to be* behind. Without being planned, it was a reawakening to my core state of being, and it motivated me to seek, touch, and inspire those who felt or experienced something like I had. I began a quest, a mission to educate and share my compassion among others who were struggling with a lack of sense of purpose or direction due to a setback or disappointment. Fear led me not, not this time. I knew that nothing and no one would pull me back to that place of lack.

I didn't have a cheerleader or a guidebook to tell me how to wake up and continue living my life, but what I did have was my own will! As humans, we have the freedom to make our own choices. So, with that, I became open, willing, and engaged with sharing myself, my truth, and my core state of being that I'd discovered through raw self-exploration. I trusted that by doing this, I could serve as a human being who was bold enough, and strong enough, to create positive changes in this world for those who *deserve* to live and experience a full life...especially those already diagnosed or would be diagnosed—and quite possibly, help them to save themselves from their own separation from love.

My desire to help came *not* for the sake of proving to be any better than *anyone* or anything else around me, but for stepping up and serving as an equal, contributing participant in this beautiful human experience. By sharing my own truth, I held faith that I would one day make a difference—to serve as a relatable soul that would prompt another human being to rekindle their own natural desire to thrive and heal by inquiring, loving, and establishing their inner self, too. I believe anyone can achieve this...if you believe that it is in your power to do so!

The way I managed to do such a thing was to first design a plan for myself. I became an engineer, contractor, designer, and calculating statistician in a gulp of breath as one heartfelt decision was made clear. I had already tried listening to everyone else's thoughts and plans for my life—guidance counselors, teachers, family members, friends...even healthcare professionals. But, ultimately, I needed to rely on myself. I learned to use my resources and connections as tools for support and guidance, but not as my Source. I decided to tap into God. When I did, I felt the direction, from Him, to go to tap into myself—my Higher Self. I had to ring the doorbell of my own mind and ask to be let in, to help myself heal.

All with perfect timing, I quit hitting the replay button of old versions and old thoughts of myself. I quit holding my thumb over the spacebar, just waiting and hoping to feel space in my world. I quit rehashing old stories. What ultimately emerged was a whole, gold-medal version of myself—finely polished, edited, and revised. I *became* a woman of depth, experience and inspiration due to my involvement with my core self and my own willingness to evolve. I began writing my own newspaper, so to speak. No outside publishers allowed, no big-name editors, no filter, no rules about how my emotions and goals would pan out as I focused on the rest (and best!) days of my life.

What my next course of action would entail was a bold endeavor that would signify my seriousness about getting to know and live out my truth. I needed a game plan for focusing my energy and time on my core value: being a woman of God, called forward to exude love, light, and inspiration to those who've lost hope or given up too soon. *There!* I said it! One sentence—one declarative sentence defining *who I am* and *what I want for myself.* I geared up and became unwaveringly passionate about reaching people who struggled like I had. My new invitation would create an opportunity for the world to see, hear and experience a beautiful, momentous second round, after being defeated in the first. So, I decided to do something that little "Lamb" would never dare to do. The artistic, music-inspired, bubbly, overcautious, diabetic Britt would compete in a *bodybuilding* competition. "What?!" My friends would scratch their heads and wonder.

Yes! An opportunity to tear down all my brick walls. An opportunity to break through fear, shame, and doubt. An opportunity to be perfectly imperfect and stand out *on purpose.* A stage. Lights. Packed seats, my medical device, tubing, tape and batteries all in attendance. Ladies and gentlemen, Brittany had finally arrived!

CHAPTER FOURTEEN

Getting to Know the Person Inside

One day after making my gallant decision, my fearless self walked into a chichi tanning salon to meet a tall, well-constructed woman who superciliously proclaimed herself to be a professional bodybuilder turned tanner. Although I didn't get what it meant to be a "professional" in the realm of holding a tube of tanning goop in something that resembled a vacuum and nerf gun combined, I went with it. "All right, she must have had her fair share of wrist turns and painting—let's see if she can paint me," I thought.

As I cheerfully walked through the door and explained my purpose in stopping by, I was stopped in my tracks by this woman whose energy field basically breathed, "I'm better than you. I know everything. I'm a pro. I am more." I sensed the arrogance and still, took one step forward. "Hi, I'm Brittany. I heard you may be able to help me. I'm looking to com..."

Before I even had a chance to finish my sentence or flash my pearly whites, I was interrupted abruptly. "You can't compete. Your thighs are too big! And what's that on your hip? You can't wear that thing on stage, they'll deduct points for that. These girls work hard—you might be better off waiting until another time or doing another show. *You* don't have a chance!" the woman reprimanded, with her hand on her hip in a side glute pose.

I looked down, forgetting about the woman I made the choice to be, and sunk back into feeling sorry for myself. "Man, I knew I shouldn't have wasted my time. She sees what I saw. She was right. What was I thinking? I should just go home and put my heavy clothes on and hide," I thought.

I tried to defend who I was and swallow my pride by explaining that I have diabetes. I cannot just eat like a bird, avoid fruit, and "cut fat" the fast way using unregulated supplements. I attempted to connect in a way that would help her see that I am a *human*, with a personality and a purpose. It felt like I was trying to persuade her to *like* who I am and *respect* that I was trying to do something powerful for those, like myself, wearing a medical device. Mentally, I pulled out the tuba, waved down the blimp, and got some big balloons to remind me of the Voice that spoke to me oh too often. "Go out and live your life. Feel radiant and beautiful from the inside out. Make imperfections more acceptable in a world that labels and judges conditions it knows little about," a voice whispered inside of me.

But despite my best efforts to have my conscious mind cheer on my subconscious mind, my attempt fell short. I waved goodbye and thanked her, even so, trying to hold an image of light and hope in myself. I couldn't help but wonder who needed more convincing that I was worthy. Me? Or a stranger?

That is one conversation, among many, that always sort of hit the gravel with me. I knew it was wrong. I realized then that it was *not* okay to be put between a rock and a hard place. Why did I convince myself that it was? Why did I give up on myself without persistence? After several visits to the mirror watching my face become beet red and my eyes green as algae, I felt pathetically judged and angry. "How could someone be so outwardly rude? Did she feel good about herself? Does she even know who I *am*?" I thought. Earlier in my life, I internalized what people around me saw from the outside and unintentionally made it who I became, but at this time in my life I *knew* better, and I wanted and deserved more for myself!

For a moment, my inner self shone through and revealed to me the old patterns of thought I was trying to learn from and improve. I mean, I couldn't throw in my own towel! "Who would help change the world to see its beauty if not me," I thought. My inner self reminded me of how far I had come to get to the point where I could and would make the decision to live my truth and become who I am divinely designed to be. I drove home pressing the gas like a kid playing Grand Theft Auto and once there, lost track of time as I stared blankly at my reflection in my bedroom mirror. I watched and felt as I experienced a bantering conversation between the two parts of myself—the rational and the emotional me. The physical body that I see, and the spiritually created body that I *can't see*, but I *feel*. When I made the mind–body connection, I was able to rationalize that it is people and comments like this that are absolutely draining, biased, and downright wrong, that plummet my self-esteem. "I am *not* going to carry that brick with me in this life! I am *free* from your words!" I proclaimed.

I thought I would get the green light. I thought I would be encouraged. I thought the people in this community would support me and help me, rather than discourage me. But I guess I was wrong. The same thoughts and feelings of not being "enough" that had defined my childhood were repeating. But why? Did I do this to myself? Was this belief something I conjured up in the ethosphere before my experience in life to "work out" a part of my life's purpose? I sought balance and answers with every conversation and replay of experiences throughout my life. It was baffling to me how twenty minutes before, I had been full of joy, enthusiastic, and propelled to do what my heart was beating without hesitation for. One conversation, with one person, pushed a faulty rewind button on the remote-control panel of my emotions and I felt utterly defeated. I didn't want to stay there, but I struggled with loosening my grip and letting go.

I closed myself off for a while, quite typical of my already established patterns. I told no one and said nothing because I convinced myself that no one would understand or care. I was meant to be a wallflower, right? That's what I told myself. I spent time reflecting on my life, its twists and turns, and how far I had come from when I was first diagnosed. I plopped down on my oversized bed, with my never-too-many inspirational pillows and a goose-down blanket to comfort my soul. "I'm safe." I thought. "I'm home. I'm protected here." As I drifted off, I caught myself having mini-dreams in a light daytime sleep. When I awoke, I remembered *why* I was lying there. I wanted, *still*, to be a symbol of positive change. I wanted to be that woman who was a role model because from pain and hurt she had finally found and established her strength. I knew other beings around this energetic sphere were just waiting for their own brave, adult hero to emerge. What this world *really* needed was some hardcore, spiritually called souls to stand up, speak up, and act, to bring a major shift of awareness to the beauty that *already* resides in our true existential creation. If I could serve as a real-life example of strength and hope to help others who struggled to see their own worth, could I serve as one of them? I set out to answer my own true life calling.

I knew that children and adults alike needed to learn how to heal the deep-rooted illusions and limitations *they* had once unintentionally created. I knew I had the power within myself to be a living example of how to create love, again, within one's self and within one's world—because I had taught myself to do so. I knew this unspoken well of happiness could be accessible to those currently living with a condition and would improve the quality of their lives. "If only they could learn what I had: the benefits of using the innate power of self-will to transform and help heal *themselves,*" I thought. My core purpose became sharpened. I would pass on the wisdom I had learned and received, that one could manifest the true living essence of the self by *loving ALL* of who you are—every cell in your body, despite what it may or may not be doing according to a textbook. It's time to express that it's OKAY to love yourself, damn it! It's okay to be who you are and not have to be fixed by anyone! We are whole—and we are enough! We already are complete, *just as we are*. Accepting that? Now, that's true healing!

I made a commitment to myself in the early hours of that evening that I would show them. I would show *everyone*. No one could tell me that I can't do it! I had had *enough*! From my childhood days of being yelled at on the soccer field by my coaches and tough-love father, I was *tired* of feeling like I was not enough. I had grown bored with the ideas I had told myself that I didn't measure up. That I wasn't smart enough, not thin enough, not popular enough, not talkative enough, not *human* enough! All of the words, comments, labels, hurtful looks and actions from my youth to my early adult years...I'd finally had *enough* of these small-minded, woefully mistaken people. I threw in my sopping towel and in an instant, a chime of thought spoke to me. It said, "Brittany, this is your time. You're going to change the world, one step at a time. Don't you *dare* give up, now. Believe in that pulsation of your heart—it will never steer you wrong!"

For the first time in my life, I was ready to buckle down and do what I needed to do, no trainers, no nutritionists, no self-proclaimed local celebrities, no arrogant people, just Brittany and her powerful mind. I was ready to get to know myself in a *whole* new way. The next morning, I felt a great sense of direction within me and made a quick phone call to the fitness facility who would be producing this popular bodybuilding show. I threw on some sneakers as I confidently pushed open the door open to reclaim my life...with more zest than I'd ever had before. Within minutes upon entering the gym, I found myself declaring, "I'm ready to sign the paperwork—I'm *in*!" I affirmed. As I signed the check and whisked my name, "B. Hines," onto the signature line, my mark was made. I was ready to make something of myself, share my imperfection, and be somebody *GREAT!*

CHAPTER FIFTEEN

Checked In and Turned On

Eight weeks away from my first big debut, I found myself reflecting on the self-motivation and discipline I had quickly adapted and made my own in order to do what had to be done. First step? I continued to strategize and re-strategize what I was doing, making realistic goals and setting clearly defined expectations for myself. I felt such clarity in doing something that was in alignment with my core values. I became invigorated by the liveliness I began feeling in myself as I experienced a natural surge of energy running through my veins. Eliminating the nightly field trip to the peanut butter jar with my large silver soup spoon was an absolute must. Especially if I wanted to prove myself and prove my point—which I did.

I found myself in modes of panic and sheer exhilaration because I'd now signed the paperwork, paid, committed to posing practice, and even given a deposit to a bikini maker. This chick would create the suit of my dreams—decked out with Swarovski bling and shine. Hey! I was my own Victoria's Secret "Angel" now! Remember those Bedazzlers that could so easily pucker stones onto just about anything, from a stapler to a denim jacket? Well, that was the era for such a business. At $350 a pop, I had *better* do my part to rock this suit and my so called "thunder thighs."

And so it began! I set out to become Brittany the nutritionist, Brittany the designer, Brittany the planner, Brittany the decision maker, Brittany the realist—and Brittany with the voice. Please forgive me if it seems as though I created my destiny out of thin air—but I had a life to start living and manifesting the dreams that had lain dormant for too long in the merry-go-round that was in my head. My time was *now*!

I decided to take my ideas and create visualizations that I knew I wanted to live out in the real world. I *purposefully* used my mind to create the life I wanted to live by spending time, yes, *time*, with my thoughts. I asked myself, "What would happiness look like, for me? How will I feel once I achieve X?" "What do I want to see when I complete X?" "What do I want to hear when I complete X?" Thoughts like these helped me to plan, build, and establish the connection with my inner self, my *true* self. Again, not a destination but a journey.

My daily practice *still* continues to strengthen upon the conversations I've held from time before. Maybe it was my favorite Technotronic hit song from back in the day (the 90s)—"Pump, pump the jam, pump it up, while your feet are stompin'!"—that kept my momentum and energy on high, but I was *ready* beyond my wildest dreams. Nothing...and I mean, *nothing* was going to stop me! Finally, I had accessed the open doors of learning how to heal through love. Through my understanding of myself, I began to release and let go of the shadow parts of myself that held me back. I had created a new vision for myself to enjoy in this life experience, and I persisted with living in this new frequency. I began listening to myself, trusting myself, and *loving* the new "song" that was my life. I understood that by actively participating in my life, I had discovered the true key to identifying and revealing my own happiness!

With an extra oomph in my step—a pep, a little jiggity dance, if you will—I began jotting down my new ideas, fit perfectly for me! I went shopping for a simple notebook, designed it to my liking, and became excited to use it to document my workouts, nutritional intake, blood sugars, and mood. *Yes!* I took notes on myself! Just like I planned and took notes to be successful in every *other* part of my life. I began cooking my own meals and became quite playful in the kitchen. I educated myself by reading and doing little bits of research to see how I could best support my goals and my energy expenditure with a healthy, safe, and diabetic-friendly diet. More importantly, I learned to use my intuition to help guide me in making the right food choices that would support my individual constitution.

Let it not go un-noted that when trainers, fitness competitors, bodybuilder pros, diabetic educators, strangers, and any other Joe Schmo felt the need to intervene and put a damper on what I was doing or how I was doing it, Brittany the realist came to pay a visit. When she did, she kindly, and respectfully, put their unwelcome comments back where they belonged—back inside their own head, of course! I gave 100% focused love and respect to myself and gave zero ability for anything less to enter the garden of my mind that I was tending to and carefully cultivating to create the best version of myself. I found my voice to speak clearly to others who thought *they* knew better and would offer their feedback or advice on how I was living my life. I showed appreciation for their "support," knowing that "I" know best, because I get my feedback straight from the Source. Brittany with the pure heart was undeniably grateful for her life experience and for *all* who supported her along the way. Brittany made it known she would do and become what she felt would best suit *her*.

My plan for living my life had now reached alignment with who I really am and what my truth meant to me. My vision matched what I felt and experienced on the inside. My ticket was purchased, luggage well-packed, and I began organizing myself and my time for my flight to my new destination! Preparation is just one aspect of *how* we use our time, make meaningful choices for ourselves, and exercise our free will to be in alignment with that of the Divine. *No one* has the ability to take away or minimize what was given to us at birth, unless we allow for it.

This insulin-dependent chick was going to do this the safe way.

Mornings, as I walked downstairs, feeling the cold wood floors of my house, I looked for opportunities to express gratitude. I found myself repeatedly looking out of my kitchen window to pray and breathe in the greenery that surrounded my home. Standing in deep thought for minutes at a time as my teakettle puffed steam into the air, whistling when it was time for me to *really* wake up and pour the boiling water over my tea bag, I was reminded of how I felt being in the presence of the *now*. Appreciating the stillness of my mind, I found my breath becoming deep, soft, and steady.

Mindful of this state of peace, I proceeded, carrying this calm energy with me as I prepared my healthy meals for the day and allowed the energy of my cheerful spirit to carry through to the food I would later digest and metabolize. (I had learned the importance of energy, and knew that *when you respect it, it respects you!)* This proved *especially* true as I explored further the relationship between food and healing in my studies in becoming a Holistic Health Counselor and Ayurvedic Nutritionist. Seeking balance in my relationship with myself and my world became a pivotal focus for me more and more each day.

I began living my life intentionally, with purpose, moment by moment. Brittany the designer created her own manageable workout schedule and daily targets. Brittany the decision maker practiced implementing a balanced schedule for her *mind* and her *body*—time for daily prayers, time for myself, time for family and friends, time for enjoyment, and time for challenging myself. I learned to reject negativity and starve myself not of food, but of outdated belief systems that were limiting or sacrificial, such as not eating to get to an "acceptable" stage weight. I grew to love the healthy curves that I once was ashamed of and tried to conceal.

I learned to question information about taking supplements or unnatural products like protein powders, enhancers, thermogenics, and animal protein, and I dismissed self-obsession. I simply embraced *life*, as life embraced *me*. Who I am, what I had, and the tools God gave me continue to keep me focused on my right path. I trusted the answers that I innately knew. I loved creating a Brittany who loves herself because for the first time in a very long time, I started to be the sole creator of the life I had envisioned. I knew I would get there, and I knew it would be a whole lot easier to become my own number one fan because God had *already* placed the blessing in giving each of His children life. I just needed to live up to His expectations. I need to learn, through time and patience, how to give, not just take. I had to learn how to listen, not just speak. I had to try, and not just give up. Only then could I understand the purpose of my real-life experience and follow the Divine plan to reach my true calling. Seamlessly, Brittany who loves herself was coming into her own—slowly and steadily, with appreciation for who she was truly meant to be.

CHAPTER SIXTEEN

Take It Off!

I'll always remember my father, from whom I always sought love and attention from (but never really felt I had received), telling me as we laid out on his Cigarette race boat to "put those friggin' magazines away, Britt." As I turned the pages of the glossy and glamorous covers of many fashion magazines, such as *Teen*, *Vogue*, and *Allure*, I fantasized about how I wanted my life to be different. For starters, I remember wanting to change my name. "Mallory Paige—what a cool, perfect name. A perfect new label for who I could be," I thought. But what I didn't realize then is that a name change, a new hairstyle, a new home, a new handbag, or a new boyfriend would never fill the void I felt in my inner world. I would, of course, find temporary relief, but I needed to get to the root of my core self to find *lasting* peace. I recognized this pattern of escapism in many of the relationships of my life—and I knew I was onto something.

When I think back, I felt an undeniable disconnect with myself. My mind, at times, seemed separate from my body, or really, the person I was invited to be in this life. I thought that by "exchanging" myself, I would be able to return "home" with more love for myself. I thought that getting the value-size candy bag of my life would be better than the one Hershey bar I had been given. I've often wondered how I would have liked myself in my younger days had I not been shown by society, over and over again, who and what *is* considered acceptable and beautiful, and what will *never* make the cover. I could just imagine what goes on in a typical meeting for major magazines and marketing while trying to uphold and maintain social standards to increase sales production: *medical device on body; not sexy; no sales; no interest; no go. NEXT!* Whatever it was, I learned quickly. Before I could even celebrate who I was, I inadvertently was taught from my surroundings what and *who* was not celebrated. My mind learned a habitual habit of resisting my true self to be what is illusory.

As I tried to protect my naturally fair skin from developing a red heat rash from the sun, I looked at the perfectly photographed models and wanted to be like them. The dainty, sleek bodies, fine silky hair, airbrushed skin, Chicklet-like teeth to match, and the most slamming outfits worn over long "thigh-gap" legs. (Yes, I've grown to laugh at that term—I'm not in that club, by the way!) I wondered why my dad had always said to put them away, when the women were so beautiful, in my virginal eyes. I would shut the magazines and mumble under my breath, "You just don't understand." Who would have thought the day would come when *I* finally did understand, in my own time of self-discovery.

As the months and weeks wound down and the competition was quickly approaching, it was time for me to get tanned up. Hopping into my new navy Jeep, I drove to a salon nearby the gym to get coat number one of five. (So *what* if my skin is white as a Dove bar? I have grown to love it. And not because someone told me to!) As I got undressed behind the curtain, I revealed the most insecure and precious part of myself—my "machinery."

"What's that?" she inquired.

"Oh, that's my sensor and my insulin pump. It helps me control my diabetes. I wear it, and I was going to keep it on for my competition. They work together to alert me when I need to take care of myself if I'm dangerously low or high. Sometimes I can't feel my low blood sugars on my own. I get hypoglycemic unawareness," I further explained.

I watched as her face stilled. I felt my heart beating as hard as the stocky boy with the mushroom haircut used to pound the drums at our middle school band concerts.

"You should *definitely* take *that* off for the show. The show is all about being glamorous; I think it might take away from your stage presence," she said convincingly.

I stood there with nothing but panties and a bra on, ready to shed all to be tainted—no pun intended. I looked at this woman's small beady eyes and her hair swishing back and forth—she made it apparent, there was no time to lose. I unhooked myself from my pump as I fought to keep a tear in my eye from falling. I was at a complete loss for words; the comments and discouraging words seemed to always surprise me when I needed strength the most. I stood bare, not just physically, but emotionally. I questioned why I was putting myself up for subjectivity and judgment. My life was *fine* and *safe* the way it was while concealing myself from the big outside world. Was it worth doing this just for some opportunity?

My arms were crossed against my chest, covering my small breasts. I looked down at my feet, fighting the fear of the *real* me being exposed. Gosh, I hated feeling vulnerable. I watched as my body became dewy, glazed, and bronzed, like I had always dreamed of. The twenty minutes of standing and turning brought me back to questioning all the avenues I'd ever taken in my life. All of the comments and feedback I had received over the years as a child and young adolescent. It was the longest twenty-something minutes of my life, as I stood motionless, waiting for the cue to twirl into what I *thought* would make me someone, something more beautiful. I said nothing. But, at the same time, I said *everything*—to myself—with no one invited to hear or critique.

"All right! You're all done! We'll spray you again tomorrow. Until then, don't touch anything, don't get wet, don't use deodorant, and don't wear a bra or underwear—nothing that can create lines. I'll see you tomorrow!" she shouted.

I put on my brother Harrison's plaid, oversized pants and a farmer-like red plaid button-down shirt that I was advised to wear to avoid touch ups later. I jumped in my car, not feeling glamorous, emotions low, and actually feeling quite pathetic. Not only did I feel sticky and smell like shea butter and a rich coconut air freshener for the next few days, but I hated who I was, *again*. I hated my diabetes! I hated having to wear something that no one understood. I hated having to explain who I am and what I have. And I was exhausted from the beeping and vibrating of the device that I had previously loved...for saving my life.

The joyful baby, the cheerful, happy girl who loved to color and do art, and be creative, and dance, laugh, and live, was undeniably lost, and had been for some time now. I had grown to inadvertently *un*-love myself. I didn't know that was actually, physically or emotionally possible. But, in my conversation with myself, I recognized a window in which I was forced to be in complete and utter stillness. My mind and my body were forced to stand still—waiting—hoping—anticipating what would fulfill me and bring me peace. I remembered the conversations I held within my mind before, knowing that my happiness would not come from being a different shade or from all the things these paid, prop-supported, and posed women in the magazines represented. My happiness needed to come from within *myself*. But, how could I learn this and get it to *stick?* How could I not only apply what I knew, but make appropriate changes in my life to keep my *new* mind track of thought *consistent*?

That night, I went home and scarfed down my favorite dinner, broccoli with marinara sauce and a piece of deliciously seasoned flounder. I had slowly become quite the chef after years of watching Mom whip up just about *everything* top-notch, from breakfast to dinner every day growing up and utilizing what I had learned in my Ayurvedic nutrition classes. After tidying up the kitchen and getting ready for bed, I slid under the covers, smiling a bit. I had nothing to laugh about, but I found that I was happy. It must've been the nurturing love I finally gave to myself to enjoy the present moment—having a beautiful family, cozy home, and warm food to come home to. It was the simple things that brought me back to the safe haven of my mind.

Saying my prayers before calling it a night, I found myself comfortably conversing, mentally, with the wisest woman I had recently begun to know. Myself, of course. I told her what I was thinking and feeling and observed where the thoughts in my mind led me next. I needed to do something to change this world. I needed to do something for the greater power of humanity, something that was real, and right. I made the decision to put my pump back on and do what made *me* feel in control of my life. I would connect with myself, connect with my ideas and my vision, connect with my Higher Power, and *yes*, connect back up technologically on both of my medical devices.

I figured I might as well feel my best and start a new wave of making beauty that is *felt*, not just *seen*. I put away the insulin shots that I had recently unpackaged and decided to slowly regain control through my insulin pump, my glucose sensor, sheer diligence, and faith that the real winner would be seen that night—devices or no devices. *Score!* The first step to healing: acknowledging my own truth! *There*. I said it! My focused energy was now reinstalled and rebooted! I felt confident knowing that I had a choice...and my choice was to take control of my life, again. Now, I could build an optimal network for myself, one filled with compassion, authenticity and strength. I was ready to compete against my old self and for all the people I *didn't* know, who were suffering silently with an autoimmune disease. Hello, tubing and tape! *Let's go*...

CHAPTER SEVENTEEN

Making My Mark

As the days turned to hours, I couldn't help but be amused that I was actually doing such a thing—a bodybuilding competition! I began to feel an authentic sense of pride about what I was doing—not only reaching for something that I had grown to love (because exercise had become routine in my maintenance of a diabetic life) but also inviting a different part of myself to surface. I was amazed at my newly renovated self. I *loved* this motivated, eager, take-me-on, don't-tell-me-I-can't Brittany! It felt like I had made a new soul connection with whom I just couldn't get enough of. It was as though I had met a dear friend, locked away within myself, whom I became eager and excited to know.

I believe everything happens for a reason, though. Maybe I was meant to go through the frustration, and through the rough patches so I could bring into existence the unbelievably vibrant and full-of-life me! It's times like this when I recognize that it's not my own will that I need. It's my absolute trust and reliance on my Higher Power—and for me, this is God. Having faith that I can create the life I envision in my mind was, and continues to be, the greatest tool that I've learned for leading a productive and meaningful life, free of fear.

I was always an organized, structured, type A personality, so maintaining a checklist of what needed to be done was imperative for keeping me on track. As human beings, we have to remember that no matter how much time and effort goes into our daily work, there will still always be more to do. Often, our mind leads us to wonder, "Am I *enough*? Have I done *enough*? Have I worked hard *enough*? Have I measured up *enough*? Have I impressed all the right people, *enough*? Have I become *enough*?" It's a never-ending conscious and subconscious tug-of-war that nobody wins...until we become fully present and aware of our core selves, as spiritual beings, too.

This was a huge breakthrough for me—accepting that it is *okay* to only do what is physically possible. By prioritizing, we can let limiting beliefs fall to the waist side and invite opportunities for the flow of life to continue, as it did when we were brought into this life. Sometimes, because many of us carry guilt or energy from the past and struggle with letting these thoughts and beliefs go, our spirit lags behind. This can cause feelings of struggle, discontent, self-sabotage, instability, and suffering. By honoring the dreams in our heart and learning to let go, we can find our true happiness through the discovery of our own inner peace. By *letting go*, we are actually *letting in* what has been lost. Rather than seeking happiness in places we have yet to find, happiness will find each and every one of us.

I kept alive my vision of happiness and dreams for my core self, while time, as it tends to do, persisted. The morning of my competition had finally arrived! As I sat getting my hair done, I listened to the sizzling curling iron and I watched my body flutter with exhilaration. My callused fingertips picked the lint off of my velour sweatsuit while I wiggled my toes in my sneakers, trying to stay warm on this blustery winter morning. Though I was nervous, simultaneously and to a greater degree my perseverance kicked in. I *knew* this was what I wanted to do. I was ready to prove what I believed in. I didn't care about the don't do's, can't do's, or will never do's—what I cared about was leaving that venue validating myself with my can do's and will do's. I knew now that despite my illness, I *am* strong! I *am* whole! I *am* complete! And *I* matter! I wouldn't give in to defeat and allow for failure—not now, not me, not *EVER!* This was for my own sake!

I sat backstage watching all of the Oompa Loompa's—I mean, tan competitors—who clearly had many fewer base coats than I did. I chuckled because for the first time in my life, I *actually* was tan and much darker than most of the women in "competitor headquarters" having such preventative care in the spray booth starting from one week before. I caught myself giggling again and again as my young-adolescent inner voice reminded me of the days in junior high when I had made my face a tiramisu of colored bronzers. Finally, at this age, and this time, I *appreciated* the color of my skin, my being, my mind, and my strength to pursue all that I was meant for.

As I waited, and waited, and waited, every insecurity I'd ever had seemed to come into my mind. I saw people glance at my medical device on my abdomen, trying to figure out what it was and why I was wearing it. No one asked. No one smiled. Businesslike faces crossed the room, tans were touched up, and resistance bands stretched across self-created boundaries as everyone fought to show their outer strength and fierceness to win. It was quite odd to see a room full of people who worked so hard just to get here and do this, yet there was little to no desire to communicate or share a smile with one another during the whole 10-hour experience. "Ego's running the show here," I thought.

I, on the other hand, sat quietly, observing and mentally recording where *I* was at this point in time. I didn't want to make this experience only about myself, because it never was. What I wanted most was to build something new—confidence in myself—and stand up for people fighting disease. Those who battle themselves...every single day. Those who *don't* have answers to a cure, but live in peace with their unrelenting questions. Those who are afraid of letting go of their tight grip, but are *willing* to build their faith, surrender, and trust in the Greater Presence that created us all. Those who, despite not having their idea of perfect health, were interested in learning how to use their *mind* to heal. I wanted to inspire others to choose to see the Light through the darkness and show how putting positive energy into their *own* self-care can have life-changing benefits. I would be a human being who shared her life story, that she was ashamed of, to bring forth positive change and inspiration for *others*. My mission became to share my *"why?"* and happily greet those waiting at the crossroads of their life—with a life changing diagnosis or choice to make—and see someone who was strong enough to open the window to life, instead of shut it. That through being who I truly am, doing the leg work, the soul work, and dedicating myself completely to my own life purpose, I could inspire others to heal and find their own, too. I have learned through my own experience that this becomes possible through one's own *accountability*.

"Bikini class, you're up!" shouted one of the big-league coordinators of the show. I gulped, holding the sensor over my stomach, and reminding myself why I was doing this. I walked in my transparent four-inch stilettos toward the stage entrance. I was a first-time competitor, and being the second woman called, with a line of experienced competitors behind me, was nerve-racking! I walked slowly behind the drapes as the first name was called. The song this competitor had chosen to play was, "We Are the Champions." I drilled my heel into the ground, anxiously waiting for my turn. "Corny," I whispered, as I lifted my eyes to watch. Soon, I turned away, remembering that I was here to run a race with myself, and *not* anyone else. I felt my knees tremble and my heart sink to my toes. It felt as if I was in the most arid of deserts, with too little air to breathe. I reminded myself that we are in a world that supplies us *all* with more than enough. *More than enough* opportunity, *more than enough* guidance, *more than enough* strength, *more than enough* happiness, *more than enough* love and *more than enough* blessings for *everybody* to enjoy. I smiled.

"BRITTAN..." Before I heard the rest of my name called, I stood, with my imagination convincing me that my feet had instantly become strapped to the wooden floor. "I can't...I'm scared...Why did I do this? I'm not ready!" I thought—and then it came. The song I had chosen for my posing routine, Enigma's "The Eyes of Truth," began to pulsate through the room. I felt my soul recharge, and the song that had resonated for me as my debut sent a chill up my spine. I lifted my head up, pulled my shoulders back, and made my entrance toward the bright lights and the judge's table. The audience cheered as I posed in the ways that I had learned would showcase my body type most appealingly. There most definitely were poses to make the most of thicker thighs and a smaller waist—I didn't have to get rid of any part of myself! I stood center stage, paused...walked to the right, paused...walked slowly to the front, paused. Then, I turned toward the back, flipping my hair to reveal my insulin pump that was strapped onto my glamorous, sexy bikini. I reminded myself to slow down, become fully present, and feel the energy of the room.

Finally, I finished my routine and delicately pointed upward with my hand. I stretched my fingertips to the sky, thanking God for the courage and power He placed in me, especially that night. "Ladies and gentlemen, Brittany Hines" rang through my ears as I walked backstage.

"Who trained you?" asked one man.

"I did," I said emphatically.

"Who did your diet?" asked another.

"I did!"

"You look great! Your conditioning is on point. You should compete in one of my shows," said an onlooker who seemed to be the mayor of all-natural bodybuilding.

"I give you so much credit, Brittany. My friend has diabetes; I know how hard it is to manage your diet, deal with the ins and outs of maintaining glucose control, *and* get where you are with performance and energy. You're amazing." Benny meant what he said. I could tell by his sincerity and the look he gave me. I guess my condition and my commitment to beat it was finally recognized and something to be celebrated. Even some people in the Never-Crack-a-Smile Club started smiling at me. I did my work in silence, knowing my message had been conveyed. Don't judge me, and let me be beautiful. Because I *still* am.

Our little fit family that we had created in just one night of being together waited behind the curtain as the winners in the top rank were about to be announced. There would also be one Overall Winner for the show. I stood, eagerly listening for and hearing the cheers from my friends and family out in the audience. The top 5 bikini girls were called out to the front. "Brittany Hines!" shouted Joe. My eyes were wide as I floated toward the stage.

I walked front and center, trying not to appear nervous as I bit my lip. As I waited and anticipated the final outcome, I wondered which number I would take home as my own. I listened to every syllable of each name called after mine and to the audience clapping as each woman left the stage without the win. When I corralled enough courage to look at how many bodies were standing next to mine, I saw just one. It was just me and one other woman who obviously had *many* years of posing and bodybuilding experience. I inhaled deeply and waited, and waited some more, until the final draw was announced.

"And the winner of this year's All-Natural Bodybuilding award goes to...*Brittany Hines*!"

I placed my hands over my mouth and bent down. My knees billowed like Jell-O, humbling closer and closer to the ground, unbelievably moved at the outcome. After all the time and energy I had spent bringing my dream to life, I couldn't believe my eyes and my ears. I couldn't believe the love and validation after all that I had surmounted.

"Go ahead ladies, please exit the stage; let Brittany have her moment of sunshine. Beauty, brains—Brittany, you have it all! Go ahead and do one more pose for us!"

I couldn't help but feel my eyes start to well up with tears, as I stood alone for a room filled with people to see me. In my most vulnerable state, I stood with just my muscular physique and my medical device clipped to the cloth of my bikini. My sensor

made a lasting appearance, too, with gluey tape stuck to my abs. I looked down as the audience rose and gave me a standing ovation. I thanked God and whispered to the most precious face in the room, "I love you, Mom."

I took home three trophies that night, along with a promise to myself that I would never give up on my Divine purpose. One trophy was for 1st Place—Bikini. The second was for Overall Winner for the bravery and inspiration of my life story. And the third trophy that I took home that night was *myself*. I knew God was with me that night as I, for the first time since my creation, valued myself as His trophy, standing bright and tall, believing, and conquering what I had feared most. I know this same power exists within each of us—and I'll show you how to discover it within yourself, too.

CHAPTER EIGHTEEN

Treading Water

As I've chosen to get to know myself better and establish a relationship with my soul, rather than look for happiness in other people, places and things, I've discovered that I have had the peace I searched for all along...inside. By trusting my inner voice, I've gained access to the wisdom that rings true for *me.* I've learned to trust myself...and my decisions. I've also learned to love, respect, and understand the building stages of life, and my own role and participation in creating the woman I always dreamed to be.

I chose to value my time, instead of fighting it...instead of blaming myself. Rather, I decided to hold myself accountable for my own life choices that I have made. By loving and accepting myself *exactly* as I am, I recognized all that I was missing. I was merely staying afloat, treading water, and my diagnosis was my opportunity to rise. It's that unpredictable, unforeseen quietness that arrives at some point in our life, in one way or another, that forces us to be alone with ourselves, and step into our true calling. It is that challenge, that break, that opportunity that asks us to reach beyond ourselves, sends a chill up our spine, and reminds us that we *are* strong. We *are* worthy. And we are called... to live fully, purposefully and intentionally, to the true desire of our heart's mission.

CHAPTER NINETEEN

The Mini-Goal Movement

As an evening of celebrating my victory came to a close after laughs and a savory meal at my favorite American restaurant, Wild Honey, all the sights, sounds, and feelings of the evening ran through my mind like a slideshow. I found myself watching and re-watching videos, looking at pictures, and recalling the words spoken to me in those special hours. What I had worked so hard for was no longer a dream, but something that had actually happened because I put in the work to make it happen. I felt captivated by the woman in the pictures—strong, humble, bold, a woman with a deeply felt sense of accomplishment.

After sleeping like a log with peace in my soul, I took the time the next morning to reflect on the things people had said to me as they were congratulating me just hours earlier. "You should be in a newspaper." "People would love to see someone like you doing something like this! "You are inspiring people with your story."

"Me? In a newspaper? I don't know about that...yeah?"

Giggles and blushing aside, Brittany with no fear came to push hesitant Brittany aside, remembering how a positive mindset had served her well before.

"A newspaper...hmm! Should I even consider such a thing? I don't know if I'm ready for that...I'd be asking too much..." There went that racetrack again. Hesitation, defeat, doubt, all flooding my mind before I took the slightest step forward. But, why?

I thought about it and thought about it some more, until the idea seemed rather entertaining. I figured, if I could muster up the strength given to me by God to simply ask, and pursue that intention with meaning, then why *couldn't* I go after another audacious goal? I put my ego to the side (you know, that thing that doesn't serve to promote growth but rather thrives on comfort, complacency, and limitations) and I focused on calling forth my inner self—the one that *is* focused on growth, maturation, courage, and strength. I knew it was my mission to ensure that I could not and would not be defeated. By making that simple decision, I created an agreement with the Universe to never give up on who I *am*.

Carving out time to acquire stillness and think about how I was going to execute this next was my next course of action. I didn't look for anyone else's approval or input. I didn't go driving around in my car, soda cans on strings tied to my bumper, honking my way through the neighborhood to alert my community that something momentous had occurred. Instead, I worked in silence. I made my goal known to God. I also made my goal *very* clear to myself. I worked with diligence and a promise to myself that I would bring this new dream, which I had just tossed the soil around and planted the seed of, into existence.

My Tetley British Blend tea bag floated around the silver spoon that clinked in my heart-decorated mug as I brainstormed ideas for spreading the message in my heart. Suddenly, it came to me. *"Aha!"* I thought. "I've got it! I love poetry, and I love to write. It's something I'm *truly* passionate about and it makes me feel like I am in my space of happiness and peace. Why not use my gift of writing to bring inspiration forth in myself and this world?"

Writing has always been an outlet for me, a way for the shy child that I *was* to be expressive. I felt freer to spread my wings with a sharp pencil in hand and a piece of paper than with verbal conversation. There it was. The goal created: I would write a poem that would share my feelings about living with diabetes and submit it for publication. I began clearing my living space to make room for the new! I threw away or recycled objects or things that I had no attachment to anymore—those that evoked feelings of denial, hoarding, or negativity. I created a clean energetic space for *receiving* clarity, freedom, opportunities, and abundance in my mind, body and spirit.

Day after day, I sat still but expectant, creating each line of the poem I would soon share. I felt space, and I *became* space. Ideas flooded into my mind like a whirlpool and I took each opportunity to seamlessly transfer them onto paper. I felt relief as I poured my heart out in a few concise stanzas that held such substance, like an absorbent crystal quartz stone. I knew I had hit another landing spot at which God would embellish my gift, with His timing and *my* persistence. I trusted that what was done once could be replicated and even enhanced, just by one simple change of thought and a clear decision. With time came my own understanding of the wisdom I held inside of my own living truth and with thanksgiving, I pressed forward!

CHAPTER TWENTY

FINDING AND FABULOUS-ING MY FOUNDATION

More often than not, I find that the conversations I have with myself upon awakening are my best ideas, and without a doubt, are the most spiritually guided. It seems as though the mind is invited and welcomed to wander, create space, and create vision beyond the world that we know, as we sleep. I've often wondered, does the whole Universe sleep, or is it just in our physical state to do so? I've grown to believe that time is limitless, and although we are taught in our human existence to monitor our appointments, the number of hours we sleep or work, or how much, or how little, time is left before our next learning experience, we never truly "stop" or "go away." We are still constantly breathing, receiving, and creating, as our thoughts become our real-life experiences in current space and time.

Still, our dreams are so fascinating that often, many of us, wake up in awe of them. We attempt to dissect their messages—the why's and what if's—and may even tell those closest to us about them, as we try to decipher their meaning. We may try to understand our "weird" dream messages. I've often tried to understand why human beings have become so comfortable with the judgment of themselves, and of others. If everyone has a mind that we each deem "ours," then why do we isolate ourselves in our thoughts, as if what we question or don't understand is wrong or by its essence secretive?

I've learned through my years of early maturation, in part because of my diagnosis of diabetes, that dreams will stay just that—mere dreams—unless they're acted on! We have the ability to bring into our lives what we really dream about—those imaginative, creative, beautiful, heaven-like thoughts that swirl in our consciousness and make us feel a type of love that cannot be seen, heard, or measured. As I put my unique feelings into words to describe the life I have gotten to know as my own, I began using the traits and attributes that have been placed inside me to better my craft.

Music and art were my first go-to choices to collaborate on my next venture. I wanted to create a poem that would lend insight to the feelings and emotions behind diabetes. When I felt the burning inside my heart to share my experience with those who may relate to it, I knew it to be genuine, almost heart-stopping. Nothing else could get done in my day until I wrote, perfected, and completed my work. Something that would make me proud to say, "I did it!"

I dreamed that I would someday write and be published. I hoped that by doing so, sensitivity and compassion could be felt in a growing society of egotism and self-obsession. I thought about how I could bring awareness to leave behind the social pressures of living through false perfection and idolization, and instead, actively live through *self-realization*. I strove to make my audience those whom felt they were "not enough" and marginalized to "be more of that." I took a big risk. But my dream became a purposeful, living reality the day I remembered to hold myself and no one else accountable for the life *I* am living. I reminded myself that love is *who I am*. "I *am* worthy!" I affirmed, strongly. I practiced telling myself a new story—and I spoke it...until I *believed* it.

Soon, I watched myself move from dream to reality. I submitted my written words to an organization that I felt would match up with my vision. Within weeks, I received an email that seemed to glow among thousands of others in my inbox. I clicked it, already feeling and knowing the response in my heart—I did it! And I *will* do it again. My poem was featured on a mainstream website to reach hundreds and thousands of viewers. It was around this same time that I was featured in the local newspaper and worldwide magazine, Diabetes Forecast. It was my time to show the strong woman I had *become*. What had once been a dream, a thought, had become my actual real-life experience. I couldn't believe this simple concept of thought preceding action. If you believe in the power you hold within yourself, you can share your own inner light, too! Just think: "What gifts can I share of myself? What impact would I like to leave on this world?"

Miracles and opportunities are accessible the minute we are ready to begin sharing the gifts inside of our heart for the larger purpose and betterment of this world. In making a choice that I would use my talents and gifts to share with others outside of myself, I began living a more purposeful, rich and vibrant life. I had fought and won the biggest battle—getting outside of my own head, and I couldn't wait to see what I would choose next, for myself and my life!

CHAPTER TWENTY-ONE

PERSISTENCE IN MY EXISTENCE

I once heard from one of my yoga teachers say that science has recognized that each of us has sixty thousand thoughts a day. That's right—sixty thousand. And ninety-five percent of them are the same thoughts we had yesterday. How crazy! And how monotonous! Have you ever taken a moment to contemplate what ideas hold steady in your mind and which of those are casually filtered to the *I'll-deal-with-you-later* bucket? I wonder what productive and fulfilling lives we all would lead if we made even a fraction of these recurring thoughts, or at least the meaningful and most advantageous ones, manifest in our reality.

Paying attention to when we are being tested is a sure way to catch our conscious and subconscious mind in the act. Thoughts are a pivotal contributing factor to our existence. Our conscience tries to keep us motivated, focused, and safe. Think about it. Everything we have, we believe belongs to *us*, as though it is *our* property, right? When it comes to the ego-centered self, everything is: *My* mind. *My* heart. *My* family. *My* ideas. *My* room. What happens when we're faced with thoughts about friendships and relationships? This is the kicker for most! These bonds can threaten the self because they're *not* all about pleasing what is considered "me" or "mine," but rather more about "we."

Are we the co-creators of our own bodies and minds? Are we strong, wise, and capable enough to respect and partake in such an important role? My belief is - YES! When we think about our presentations of ourselves and how we are perceived by the world, it is important to pay attention to the thoughts and feelings we hold inside our mind. These connections or guided directions can help steer us in the right direction and catapult us into living our best lives! What or who is stopping *you*? Take some time to think about the things that people have told you that you can or cannot do and then the things *you've* told yourself you can't do. More often than not, you will see you will have created your own laundromat and invited everyone else to send you their dirty laundry.

We are created and delivered into our world with a uniqueness and spirit unlike that of any other. Have you ever met anyone who was the spitting image of yourself? Someone who spoke the same, laughed the same, looked the same, dressed the same, weighed the same, exhibited the same mannerisms? I didn't think so! That's because our being, our spirit, is placed inside of us at birth, but it is our *experiences* and *thoughts*—our *vibrations*—that are sent out to the Universe to become our powerful existence. These vibrations present us with the opportunities we experience in daily life. It can be overwhelming to take this all in. But just like when your more seasoned elder put their hand on your shoulder when you were a kid and said, "You are what you eat" or "You are what you say you are," there is substantial truth to this.

Some days your body may ask for rest—especially if you're living with an autoimmune condition or some other circumstance. Other days, hopefully the majority of days, your being may be sent a flood of power, fuel, and motivation to get on with it and keep on truckin'. Even when there are things to do, there may be times when you really won't feel up to answering the call of your 365-days-a-year secretary or your inner voice (who takes no vacation days). However, ignoring that small voice inside you is like speeding through the yellow light on a traffic camera. You might think you're winning by racing and ignoring them, but eventually, you'll have to face it.

To avoid such frustration, instead of feeding your appetite

for procrastination by sifting through your mental file cabinet of ideas and things to do, *capture the moment*. Pull out that tangible to-do list and find an option that's more fitting for your current mood. Choosing to ignore your 365-days-a-year secretary could derail you from making the most of an opportunity! This little voice naturally and eloquently sends feelings to our spirit when we are willing to receive them. This is when God speaks; thoughts of inspiration. So, procrastination, in simple terms, would be its complete detriment. Procrastination wants you to stay in a space of no action and no decisions—therefore; no movement. You wait...and wait...and wait...until the "perfect time" or until too much time has passed, while your mindset and personal growth are stalled in their tracks. By putting your inner guide *first* in line, you can ensure that you're feeding yourself with the right intention, for the right purpose, so your Higher Self can shine through.

As I slowly and consciously began welcoming my inner 365-days-a-year secretary into my spirit, I recognized that the inspiration I felt never would have developed into the vision I hold today if I had chosen to irrationally escape from it and ignore my truth. My thoughts, dreams, and desires have become an immediately gratifying, tangible, relatable piece of work that no one (myself included!) would ever have gotten to enjoy, had it lain dormant, stuck inside my head.

I've recognized that by opening our minds to the inner guidance that we each equally and undividedly receive, we can become the co-creators and facilitators of our own destiny. How about that for one of your sixty thousand thoughts today? Be persistent. Be present. Most of all, be open. Be open to the love and opportunities the Universe has created for us *all* to enjoy and embrace. We are *meant* to be whole and happy. We are fully supported. We are *alive*. We are created with *extraordinary* gifts inside of our souls. Why not let go of holding onto all that is perceived as "ours" and listen to the wisdom that speaks from inside?

CHAPTER TWENTY-TWO

A Spa-like Experience

Have you ever needed to escape the noise and conversation inside your own mind? I think about the efforts I have unintentionally made throughout my life to block out that inner voice. I have had to spend a substantial amount of time practicing *how to know* this person inside of me, in this body, and *how* to love her. For many of us, gravity pulls us out of ourselves, somehow, and we never learn how to reel ourselves back in, unless we *try*. We are constantly molded to look to outside circumstances and people to fill our tank of happiness. Why not take the initiative to search for our own happiness through really getting to know the person *inside* of the physical body? It's possible, so why do we make it so that it seems so...impossible?

Maybe our true happiness lies not in the outer world and all that "we" have created to be "ours," but rather in seeking that pure contentment and peace through questioning, listening, and responding to the inner being. This simple shift in self-understanding would enable each of us to live in a world from which we are not trying to escape, but rather *fully live*.

I began refocusing my mind to do exactly this—live fully and live *NOW*. By doing so, I naturally began to see that life is *so* beautiful—there is no need to escape. This feeling can be quite common for most of us, as monotony seems to become intolerable. The desire to want to leave or just up and go may arise, but if you are one seeking to break the old patterns based on fear or the ego, it may be worth your while to examine your very own relationship with escape.

Ingrained in us, somewhere, seems to be the notion that we must *earn* love. We don't, or we can't just *get it*. Somewhere along the line, many of us learned that love is something we have to work for. We have taught ourselves we must be "worthy of love." I'll share a time I was reminded that love is *who I am* and not what I do or do not have. On my best friend Meryl's bachelorette weekend, we visited a day spa to enjoy a girls day. When we arrived at the spa, I walked up the stark staircase and was greeted by well-manicured staff and the fresh, clean scent of lemon. As I swiped my card to pay for a day of relaxation, I inquired about the treatments, such as foot rubbing and massages. "One hundred and seventy-five dollars for the facial," Letty said. That was all I needed to hear. Nodding and smiling politely, I decided to pay for access to the pool and sauna buffet instead of doing a treatment. They had a variety of pools and saunas to choose from and I could jump in any one of them. That did it for me! "Bring on the water beads, baby!" I thought.

Our very giddy group of gals waited to be searched before we were allowed in. There it was. The big, shiny sign: "NO FOOD OR DRINKS ALLOWED BEYOND THIS POINT." The red X's through each item on the sign brought butterflies to my stomach, knowing I was going to have the search warrant police coming through. (Diabetics always carry food—you just *always* have to be prepared!) Big bag and all, there I went, placing my load on the glass table for the purse police to make sure I wasn't bringing in a turkey dinner, causing them to lose business.

"Oh no, ma'am. This is *not* coming through. You're gonna have to throw all this out. I can't allow this!" a woman in uniform said in an impressively deep manlike voice.

"But, I'm diabetic, I have Type 1 diabetes. I follow a very strict diet plan and need to have food or juice with me at all times, in case I have low blood sugar..." I attempted to explain.

"No Ma'am. We deal with people like you all the time, and they're fine. You can leave it here with me. You're not getting through with all these snacks. This is too much," she persisted.

I wasn't going to give up on myself. "Can I please speak to a manager?" I inquired.

As I began to feel the rush of blood to my cheeks, a short "official" looking man with slick, gelled back hair and a name tag approached me. He had that "I'm just doing my job" face on. I swallowed my hesitation and began speaking, explaining my medical needs, while simultaneously looking for a glimmer of heart.

"You can take the elevator down from the eighth floor to the first floor and your snacks will be waiting right here for you," he explained.

"Sir, with all due respect, if I have low blood sugar, I need to have my food *with* me; I won't have time to push the down button, wait, come down seven floors and stroll here to get my snacks. I need fast-acting carbohydrates like juice, rice cakes, or raisins, *immediately*. This is simply a matter of...do you want me to have my few snacks concealed in my purse or risk that I pass out in your facility because you won't let me by with my medical necessities?"

With dismay and a soldier-like impassiveness, he looked at me. "Ma'am, I will make an exception, but I will have to ask that if you must eat, you hide yourself so no one else can see. You know, because I don't want other guests to think that it's okay to have food beyond this point."

"No problem. I will hide it." I looked away. The old feelings about myself started to creep in. I tried to *still* love myself, but it was hard to.

"We have locker rooms and restrooms..." he assured me.

"I will eat in a stall if I have to," I replied. I half smiled and walked past the gate, where the purse police stood, watching my every move. "Thank you," I said quietly, and looked down at my feet as I approached the women's locker room. My enthusiasm for fun had been sucked out of me and I felt alone again, even though I was surrounded by hundreds of relaxed people. "No one gets me. No one is wearing a medical device on their abdomen like me. No one has to explain who they are. No one has to carry all this food wherever they go. I am different. I hate being me," I thought.

As I watched the crowds and my own group of ladies giggle, admiring each other's freshly manicured fingertips, and doing the things that girly girls do, I felt weighed down and wished there was someone like myself who could relate or understand. I caught myself daydreaming about a spa with stands of glucose tabs made of ice cream and frozen chocolate bonbons at every spiral staircase landing. There would be stands with chilled, freshly folded washcloths to help with the sweatiness that low sugars often cause. (Let's get real: my imagination was working overtime!)

I guess my daydream was leading me to understand my desire to create a world *way* more friendly and inviting to diabetics and people who live their life...differently. I walked through spa rooms full of bikini-clad women. I felt more comfortable in my fuzzy polar-bear robe. Why would I want to expose my scar tissue, tape, tubing, and gadgets after now having to hide myself? My best friend, Melly, who is so supportive of me shouted across the reflexology heated walk path, "Brittany! Take off your robe! Look, no one's wearing their robe here." I looked up, entertaining the idea, but knowing that even she could not understand how vulnerable I felt.

The party-bus girls twirled their hair, laughing and gallivanting as they giddily approached each sauna variety—Infrared, Pink Himalayan, The Icebox—they all had snazzy names. I waited outside because I knew the sensitivity of my body while on insulin. I knew better than to think a room that was over 115 or below 0 degrees would be conducive to controlling my glucose numbers. "I'll be relaxing in the lounge, guys," I called out, trying to exude happiness and confidence (as if this was what I preferred to do).

I complied with the "QUIET ZONE" sign on the window and sat still as my mind wandered. *I* wanted to be out. I wanted to be *out*! Out of this body, out of this place, out of this gigantic Jug-O-Judgment I could never seem to avoid. I began to pray.

Hours passed and I knew I was running low on snacks and test strips from testing so frequently. Danielle, Meryl's triplet sister, kindly texted the car serviceman Enrique and asked him to bring the car up so I could pick up some more from my travel bag.

"He'll be here in ten minutes, Britt," Dani shouted.

"No problem! You guys go ahead and eat. I'll wait for him!" I said.

All the girls considered what they could and would have for lunch—the steak and salad taco bowls, the dumplings, the dough balls to be shared, the churro-bagel that was so big it could be worn as a floatation device in a swimming pool. Oh, the options! Oh, the variety! Oh, the freedom! I smiled. "Oh, yum! That sounds good; you'll enjoy that!" I said enthusiastically.

"That smells good," I said.

"You can't have this though, right? Like, diabetic shock! Hahaha," they cackled. They must've thought this was something funny to joke about. I didn't laugh.

"Yeah, no. I definitely can't eat stuff like that," I said, as I played piano with my toes. Before more smells and chat-chewing occurred over questions such as "safe versus not-safe" food, I found myself naming some things I used to enjoy and explaining why they no longer made the cut on my shopping list. Talking "diabetes talk" as I call it, made me feel good. Simultaneously, it encouraged me to reflect on just *how* much knowledge I had acquired about living with this disease. Something that I never really gave myself credit for. Still, I felt like there was so much more for them (and the world) to know. But, would they care? I cut my spiel short and excused myself to go pick up my goodies from Enrique's truck. I was thankful I had my own "happy" meal, one that I had prepared with love, for myself. Steel cut oats with coconut water, unsweetened soy milk, and cinnamon (great for circulation and achieving lower glucose ranges). Delish *and* safe!

I pressed the elevator button firmly as I listened to what felt right and what made me most comfortable. I walked with purpose and good vibes, made possible by diligently responding to the needs of my soul. I guess you could say that *that* was the best dessert—feeling better by giving my body what it needed, self-care and self-love. How's that for a dash of sweetness?

CHAPTER TWENTY-THREE

The Conversation

What if I were to tell you that scientific research shows that our conscious mind uses only ten percent of our brain's capacity? The other ninety percent is floating uselessly inside us, so to speak, taking in all that we see, hear, smell, taste, and touch. It's amazing to me that these subconscious impressions hugely influence what we attract or do not attract into our lives. We become *what we think*.

Many of us have formulated beliefs, judgments, and preconceptions before we even celebrated our first birthday. Our life experience will try to teach us the things we need to know or understand about our true self and our life purpose through our family, relationships, celebrations, challenges, disappointments, and choices. Becoming a learner of life, a student of life, and understanding this in my own experience, I chose to become accountable and present in my daily living so that I could create a framework for my future. The past is over, but I recognized its influence: my thoughts are products of everything that I've added to my backpack of "stuff" throughout my life.

My family background—one actively involved parent, my mom—provided a perfect atmosphere in which to learn to love myself. I had to *learn* to love *all* of me, despite the lack of love I felt from my father in my upbringing. I later understood the value or degree to which I felt worthy of love had *nothing* to do with the amount of love I did or *did not* receive from other people in my life that were around me. These relationships served as mere lessons for me to learn more about myself than I ever could have on my own. For this, I am beyond grateful.

Additionally, the diagnosis of my diabetes gave me a reason to take care of myself, with no room for procrastination. My uncertainty about developing trust in my friendships and relationships, constantly being in escape mode, eventually guided me to develop my faith and my trust in God. It also taught me how to trust *myself* and the unfolding of my life purpose. Were these coincidences or just a call for me to align myself to the plan of the Universe? After much soul searching, self-help, and time spent being a learner and observer of my own self, I strove to spend time fixing my old patterns and beliefs of feeling like I had nothing, when I truly, already, had *everything*. I had more reason to look at my inner world than at my outer. Despite the countless conversations, self-help books read, and workshops taken to "just *be*," I was looking for answers from everybody *except* the person I knew best—*myself.*

As easy as it was to convince myself it wasn't and never could be what I was missing or who I didn't have in my life, I finally recognized the real void was the time I spent ignoring my true essence. It wasn't the clothes in my closet or the number of swipes or likes I could or could not get on social media. It wasn't the makeup tutorials I didn't watch, the exercise I did or didn't do that day, the boyfriend who did or didn't love me, or the father who didn't have time for me. It was an understanding of *myself* that I didn't have. Therefore, no other relationship, degree, handbag, fancy outfit, diamond, or vacation could give me the value or gratification I always hoped I would one day discover. It was just me and my *mind*—and until I fixed my thoughts, my life would never *feel* complete. I developed what I had already come to know and recognize: I *AM* worthy of loving myself, and I wanted more than anything to put in the work to make it happen, and last.

I woke up the next morning with a chunk of Post-it Notes

next to my bed. I wrote reminders of the self-loving thoughts that I would tell myself every day. I started the day with an extra-peppy bounce in my step, determined to try and figure it *ALL* out—the meaning of my life, the reason I had gotten sick, why I just couldn't find happiness, despite having it all, and what I could and would do about it *now.* I spent time meditating on how to grow from my past and evolve as a wise, strong, active participant in my own life, emerging as a young woman coming into her own. Life loved me! It was my time to *believe* it.

I thought about what I wanted. I wanted the advice of everyone who walked before me, who'd been there before me, who'd cried in a hospital bed like I had, who'd felt the pain that I had felt. I wanted to feel related to. I wanted to feel understood without having to express or revisit the painful events of my life. I couldn't help but think about myself and of all the stories I'd convinced myself were true. Slowly, I began to let go, releasing each limiting thought, belief and memory that I tightly clung to. I planned the new direction of my life after revisiting these memories and unlocking the power they held within me. I thought about my quest for freedom, determined to find it, right here, right now—believing it wasn't anywhere else but *here inside of me.*

As I sat on my magenta buckwheat yoga mat, I straightened my spine to connect myself to the Universe. (For newbies to meditation and mindfulness, this means creating a sacred space that you call your own, surrendering, listening and receiving the information that comes forth). I didn't always have an agenda for what I was asking for, but I knew that just by carving out time in my day to be still and listen, I would understand what I *needed* to know. By connecting to my Higher Self—my subconscious mind—I became aware of my actions and reactions in the present world.

Fall turned to winter and soon, winter turned to spring. My world became one of two dimensions merged together that I would later appreciate in my attempts to guide my distracted mind in the direction of sound thought. I decided to follow where I was being led, trusting my soul and the lightness I felt, and knowing what was undeniably becoming my truth. I grew clear in my desire to share hope, faith, strength, courage, and inspiration as my healing began and my new story was being created.

It is our own comparisons of what we are, to what we are not, that determine our identity—who we are in this world. Subconsciously, we measure our worth based on our perception of ourselves and our perceptions of others. It is in our self-talk that we have the chance to become aware of our thinking and fix any undeserving judgments, immediately. In simple terms, if our thoughts are loving, peaceful, and intentional, then they will be reflected back to us in that same way. Similarly, if one's self-talk is hurtful, demeaning, or judgmental, then our experience of life will mirror just that.

I've found that human beings find gratification through feeling *validated*. We like to know that our thoughts, our ideas, and our presence are accounted for, giving rise to the idea that we *are* somebody. This mere belief brings us a great deal of satisfaction to pursue deeper, meaningful opportunities in our lives. Even something like judging who has less or more than we do distracts us from the thoughts about *ourselves* that we often try not to deal with. Again, the problem lies not in others, but in our own minds. The glorification of others, the judgment, and the comparisons to others must stop if we are to light a new wick for our own candle, our own lives, and our own plans.

Instead of denying our true self and fighting what we are given by pursuing other things, other people, and other answers, our lives may be so much more harmonious if we simply learn to *value* our inner voice and its guidance. This fight-or-flight existential response is what many people ride on to avoid dealing with their reality and the things in it that can be considered "tough." Doing this day in and day out may satiate us, for a little while, distracting us from thinking deeply and appreciating what is *real*. If we keep filling up that racetrack car with gas, soon the monotony, complacency, and replication will exhaust and bore our creative natures. We will find that from one relationship to the next, one job to the next, one purchase to the next, one home relocation to the next, we are *still* dissatisfied. The only way to move ahead is to actually *look back* at the thoughts you've held about yourself. By stretching yourself through your ability to really get to know and understand your life experience and what it has taught you about *yourself,* you can then begin to accept and love who you are. Through practicing this, you will be actively moving toward a renewed lens, establishing your receptiveness and capacity to grow from your experiences. We are much stronger and *so* much more capable than we believe.

My genuine desire to exit the boxing ring of competitive, attachment-based life was what empowered me to run my own race. I set a routine must-do: speaking to myself. *Who was I? What was important for me to tell myself?* Speaking, silently or out loud, no matter how odd it may seem, *works*! It is a helpful way to understand yourself, and the thoughts you are currently telling yourself and therefore are living and believing. It provides a time for you to reflect on yourself and gain insight as to where you see yourself going and create a path for it to happen. Making space for *yourself* allows you to make space in your life!

Turning my face to the cool side of my pillow each new day I began asking Universe to guide me toward whatever it was I needed to tackle that day. Before I ate each of my meals I would check in with Universe and ask, "Will this food help my body heal?" or "Will my body respond positively to eating this _______?" I paid attention to the signals my body was sending. I watched as my body spoke to me, not in words, but through feelings. Sometimes I would receive a deep knowing just by feeling chills instantly sent up my forearms. Other times I would see a symbol in my mind. In this way, I was able to listen, learn and respond in a way that was in *my* best interest. When the answer did not come immediately, I knew it would come and to look out for it. Who would've thought the best conversations would lead me to observe new thoughts, feelings, and knowledge through my own senses? Maybe I could use my inner voice to provide a manual for self-healing. If I *thought* I could, then I knew I would—and so, I began.

I began asking my 365-days-a-year secretary what my next step should be in taking care of myself, to heal. There would be a lot to *un-learn* and for me to *re-learn*. I trusted the subtle communication my body provided me, paying close attention to the synchronicities, and my daily experiences that would help shape me into the healthiest and best version of myself. This feeling of being guided, supported, and loved by what I don't see, but know and feel, continues to be one of the greatest blessings I have come to experience in this life. If we choose to embrace our inner Light which created us, we have the opportunity to expand ourselves and understand our larger purpose in this beautiful circle of life. Reprogram your mind for what you want and watch as you re-mold your subconscious vision for yourself and your life! It's the best relationship you can form, and one you will have your entire soul journey.

CHAPTER TWENTY-FOUR

Holy, Holy, Happy

With my conscious desire to remold my thoughts, I asked Universe for a sign that I was being heard. Universe spoke to me—but it wasn't until I was ready to hear its messages that they came through clearly and openly. Feeling as though sparkles of inspiration were showering me with freckles of love, I received the message that came softly to my mind: "You must be happy in order to heal." I felt my spine straighten and tears stroll down my face as my body became enraptured on my yoga mat.

When I opened my eyes, I felt like my biggest secret had been broadcast over a loudspeaker. I couldn't believe that the Universe knew my *real* secret. I was *still* carrying thoughts and feelings of unhappiness that I had taken on since my diagnosis. I still had left over resentment from my childhood days of feeling unloved by my father. I was reminded that the *self*-love part of me had never fully developed because I was too busy trying to do everything to make everyone else happy—my parents, boyfriend, teachers, colleagues, friends, and family. Although I fully *enjoyed* doing this, I knew I couldn't hide the "I'm happy" card any longer. I couldn't *only* take care of the people around me so I could escape my own head. I needed to care for my own self, too!

As I internalized the words of Universe, I became curious to discover my own route to happiness, wherever it might lead. I decided to transcend my fears and spend time with my core self, allowing my Divine spiritual path of self-understanding and growth to unfold before me. I embraced the old me, welcomed the new me, and spent time practicing forgiveness—to myself and to all. I cried hearty cries and got down on both knees, sometimes several times a day. I became humbled by my entire life experience as snapshots of my life scrolled through my mind. I began changing not the things I saw, but how I perceived life itself, and my experience in it. I was ready to turn inward for some real, heavy-duty, self-love and exploration. Prayer became my focus as I designed a "mindful workout," which consisted of fostering creativity *within* myself and *outside* of myself. A balanced sleep schedule, wholesome foods, like-minded friendships, establishing healthy relationships and creating new visions for the life I dreamed would all be where it would *start*. Spirit opened my lips as I, somewhere, out of mid-air began to sing my favorite Madonna song, "You must be my Lucky Star - 'cause you shine on me wherever you are..." I knew this was just the beginning, but I'd hit my holy happy!

CHAPTER TWENTY-FIVE

Thinking Up

Being an introvert is like being a pinata...full of ideas, creativity and unique gifts, yet waiting for one big final*"ta da!"* moment to be discovered and revealed. I take advantage of the opportunities that prompt me to question myself, asking myself, "What am I judging right now?" or "Why am I assuming something that I know nothing about?" I learned to use my mind as a tool, training it to be receptive to the feelings and energy I receive from the people, conversations, music, and events throughout each day. I'd become quite comfortable with self-talk at this point, so I embraced each window of opportunity to catch myself in my thoughts and work my new knowledge and awareness for my favor.

From practicing this awareness, I learned to see patterns and self-created beliefs that had become part of my identity. "They're all wearing open-toed shoes. I'm wearing boots. That was stupid. Why would I think I should be wearing boots in March?" I quickly fixed these hindering thoughts. I had to be sure to catch myself in these moments when my ego tried to spill out judgments that were unaccepting of choices I'd made. I recognized how incredibly insecure I had been. I began using this knowledge to set *new* pathways for myself. When I caught my mind in the act, I quickly corrected it, and redirected it, affirming "It's okay!...I *still* love myself. I know I made the best decision for *me.*" As I corrected my thinking, the thought passed. I immediately felt a sense of freedom. My conscious role was to conduct conversations in my mind that were consented to by my Higher Power, and not to allow room for anything else.

I decided that if the conversation was not meant to move me, inspire me, or push me to make myself stronger, better, or wiser in some way, I must immediately close the mental shutters. This would prevent old patterns of piling and stuffing expendable emotions into the mental cabinets of my mind. I wore a smile that revealed a willing spirit as I chose a mindset of hope and faith. I consigned my yesterdays to the past. What I hope to convey to you is this: life will be beautiful if you allow beauty to reside in your consciousness. Life will be joy, if you choose to invite that energy of love and enlightenment into the things you do! This kind of relationship with yourself will empower you to attract the thoughts you are creating and believing. If you can step out of your own head, even for a few moments, you will feel the beating of your heart letting you know that you're *still* here—*still* so alive and *still* full of unlimited potential. Choose the direction of your thoughts and choose the direction of your *life!*

CHAPTER TWENTY-SIX

The Conscious Choice

My journey has taught me to accept my queries and not to need or seek explanations , but finally, to accept who and what I *am*. I found laughter to soften my soul, and I looked for experiences that brought me sweet joy. I *purposefully* and *intentionally* planned my new life story. I knew that the Brittany who was emerging was *so* much more dynamic and well-versed than the Brittany that had been. Reflection became an instrument to which I would seek, establish, and live out my own desired destiny. It was *my* ability to commit to releasing fear, doubt and worry that empowered me to lead the life I had always dreamed—and deserve! Eventually, it all changed. The life of feeling as though I had no direction or purpose became a hazy blur the moment I began pressing into my faith, speaking prayers from my heart, and sitting in silence with the woman I was *all* along. Eventually, I understood why I was called...to rise higher.

Little had I known that God was quietly performing a work in me, and creating the sequence of events that were necessary if I were to step into the person I was meant to become. The next phase of my life, with chronic illness, would never have become the opportunity for me to heal had I chosen to fight it. The diagnosis was a little seed of learning and of love. It was Universe's invitation for me to take accountability, responsibility and action in my own life to recreate the vision I had of myself and my world. It was my choice to learn how to rescue *myself.* My willingness to *find* me again came through learning how to love *who I really am*.

CHAPTER TWENTY-SEVEN

RSVP-ing "Yes" to My Life

Once you find yourself willing and able to surrender, you may question: "Well, where do I go from here?" The first step is to begin by investing in *yourself!* Spend time revisiting the parts of yourself you haven't given much of your time or energy to, because it was easier to "forget." Those parts of you that in silence, you feel called to bring forth and heal. For many, it is sometimes easier to just live vicariously through someone else. Maybe the pain is just too deep to tolerate. Alternatively, maybe we just have become too accustomed to numbing who we really are and what our priorities are. By creating this space to become vulnerable, you will begin to release the self-inflicted thoughts you have created in your own mind.

Believe it or not, it seems that our casual relationships and conversations—"I met them at a party one time"; "We sat next to each other in math class"; "I used to date his friend"—occupy most of our mental inventory! Tell me if you agree, but, the majority of our most replayed conversations and interactions tend to be with people whom we barely even know—near-strangers, friends of friends, or people we have invested in briefly, such as a boyfriend or girlfriend. In these types of interactions or connections, it's often the non-verbal communication we pick up on, as an energetic exchange is shared versus an actual deep connection. With this, our mind may tend to wander, guess, and even make assumptions based on our own preconceived ideas—

not necessarily truth.

On a mission to recognize the purpose of the soul inside my body, I stepped inside myself more and more to become a person living with purpose. I set out to search for what is beyond mundane acceptance. The name of the disease is what I have, but it is not *who* I am, I realized. The pancreas is what I have, not *who* I am, I remembered. The diagnosis is what I have, it's not *who* I am, I accepted.

Leaving behind the thoughts and decisions of a life of limitation, guilt, and shame, I chose a different path for myself. I didn't hope that what I had would go away, but rather made a dignified effort to truly understand the core of who I am. That way, the details of my life's journey would lead to an understanding of my whole body. I couldn't bear the thought of placing a lock on the door of my life, never to be opened. I had found my key, and now, I was ready to return "home."

My purpose became clear the minute I stopped blaming myself. I moved in synchronicity with what felt right for me—moment by moment. My destiny was waiting for me! I knew if I could tap into this gift that I had, develop it, strengthen it, and use it, I could better myself and better this world. I discovered that I would spend time gathering information about the root cause of all disharmony by connecting with my intuition and my Higher Self through the power of Universe.

I was guided to teach through example, healing through the power of the mind. To inspire those feeling and living in a stuck mental state to choose the "Submit" button on their application for living a full life, rather than to click "X" to exit out. I was ready to get to know the sole purpose of the soul that steers intuition, guides and protects the human condition. I would devote my time, energy, and life experience to help others learn to heal, too, through self-love, reflection, change, consistency, and *willingness*. I'm sharing my light because I witnessed what happened when I RSVP'd "Yes" to my life!

CHAPTER TWENTY-EIGHT

Me + 1 = Maybe

The thing about an invitation is that usually there is some sort of plan or event that ignites excitement about bringing a group of people together. When I speak about inviting someone into my life, that person is *myself*. I'm talking about making another *(yes, another!)–deliberate* decision. After years of hiding and disconnecting from the world, I made a choice to *live* my life and blossom into the person I was meant to be. I needed to *participate* in my life and not be a bystander. This choice involved not just myself, but also, friendships and relationships. Sure, I was nervous. I mean, I had done my share of dating. I did the three-dater, the one-weeker, the two-monther, and the no-wayer. I even fell in love when I didn't love myself—what a mistake that was! But it made for great storytelling and prompted me to decide how I wanted to dive into this interconnected world, as an adult, emerging as a better and stronger woman.

I had uninvited myself from what we, as humans, should be able to experience as part of our birthright—joy, fulfillment, love, worthiness, and a feeling of peace. Aware that my life was passing me by, I recognized how uninvolved I was in my own life. I was merely *existing*. "Not anymore!" I proclaimed. Life is so exciting when you're not just viewing it from a park bench or as a museum exhibit! There were some major mental, emotional, physical, and spiritual shifts that were being uprooted through my meditative practice and it felt *amazing* to be in the process of purging myself clean. Survive? I am ready to *thrive*!"

I signed up for a life-progression/therapeutic betterment course that gave me yet another opportunity to look at myself in the mirror and dig deeply into the woman inside this body. After showing up for myself mentally and physically, I caught myself looking into a mirror during one of our class exercises. For the first time, I felt as though I was seeing the embodiment of my soul.

For a moment, I viewed my physical body merely as a costume that I had put on, and saw my *self*—a beautiful soul existing, rather than just my physical body. It was in this time that I had an *aha!* moment, which I will never forget. I found myself gazing into my eyes for a number of minutes, losing track of where time went. As I stared at the person I had lost along the way, I couldn't help but feel the difference from all the other times I got ready and viewed myself in a mirror. This morning was different... because for the first time in my life, I recognized the beautiful person I had always *wanted* to see. I connected to the soul of who I was deep inside, but never knew, until now!

The day that I invited myself to be a part of my physical existence, was the day I began to see change in my life and become an active participant in my own life. My journey toward becoming the best version of myself was happening. Not only was I there to take part, but I was able to appreciate and witness these wonderful opportunities that were coming to pass as a part of my life experience. I began to actively know and understand my *soul*.

I am often asked, "How did you do it, Brittany? How did you get to where you are now?" Although it is flattering, I'm sometimes quite baffled at these questions. Maybe they haven't learned of the power they hold within themselves, yet. Maybe they have yet to discover their own secrets, too. If you are someone ready for great change, deep soul-searching discovery, and complete empowerment—if you feel ready to trust the plans that are already set forth by Universe to step into your truest self,

I am here to tell you that exactly what I'm doing is completely accessible to you, too.

My transformation process came from a desire to change myself, and my world, for the better. I decided to charge my own will, with that of Universe, to create the life I wanted to live—not necessarily the one I had unintentionally created in the movie screen of my mind. My renewed sense of self became the light of my eyes—the child I had not yet given birth to, the house I had not yet lived in, the relationship that I dreamed of, the career that I had felt so driven toward—all that was what I envisioned. I set my intentions clearly, and patiently waited as they took root. I took deliberate action to bring these dreams to the forefront of my mind, and ultimately, into my physical world.

I drew it in my mind with a fine-tipped black Sharpie pen. My new mantra became "I *am* lovable and I *am* worthy of being healed!" I believed it, I believe it, and I continue to make it a tangible, discoverable, and perceivable verity. I focused on inviting myself—physically, emotionally, and spiritually—to become fully present in the main event, which *is* my life! It became my divine purpose to know, love, and accept myself as much as the Divine loving Source, who created me. I made a conscious decision to love myself and be in connection with God, every single day, to know *His* will for me. I was eager to practice this *awakening* and to be open to messages that came from within.

CHAPTER TWENTY-NINE

How to Converse with Your Universe

The Greek philosopher Diogenes once said, "We have two ears and one tongue so that we would listen more and talk less." This quote is so powerful. Sometimes the things we need to hear are not always what we want to hear. Still, what we hear, say and do all encompass what we think, and therefore; how we live. I thought I had my life mapped out, while waiting for life to find *me* each day. Unlike now, I used to allow every interaction or situation to affect my mood. This would inevitably have an impact on my self-talk. I later realized that the *energy* I felt was the result of internalizing what had taken place *around* me. Holding onto these thoughts or feelings is what would lead me to feel more inclined to tune out the world and become immersed in the static of the day's events *or* become incredibly motivated by my daily accomplishments and run with it. Clearly, the latter was a choice more beneficial, positive and healing for me than the former.

Despite not having all the answers or the "perfect prayer," I began to appreciate my full-hearted efforts. I became directly connected to my whole self, expressing my thoughts, visualizing my dreams, speaking from my heart center, and connecting with the Universe to build my reality from the inside out. I placed hope behind my intentions and trusted that someone or something greater was listening—whom I couldn't see, but could feel. I began to love the relationship that I was seeking, with what seemed unfamiliar, but also comfortable and inviting. It made me think: "If I can feel such peace with what I don't see, what else is possible that I am not seeing?" I wanted to strengthen my relationship and connection with what I knew to be all around me—*LIGHT*. My little every day miracles began showing up the more I surrendered and simply aligned my soul with its purpose.

Where have you found your own Light? Who has presented themselves in *your* life that has given you a push when you needed it most? What lesson did you learn in their presence? What *values* have you gained from your experience with that person or situation?

Take some time to jot down the people in your life who have led you to a place of deep connection or happiness and what each has brought you. Some questions for self-discovery and learning are:

- What was going on in your life when they entered it?
- How long did this relationship last?
- At what point did the relationship no longer serve you?
- What challenges or trying times have you encountered?
- What keeps coming up for you?

Think about the *lesson* you learned. Identifying whether there is a particular pattern or feeling will help you to understand part of your own life-work in your very own journey.

CHAPTER THIRTY

Wake Up, Refresh, Renew

Knowing that I now had the life experience and the acquired knowledge to demonstrate to others how to take better care of themselves—I knew I could be the living, breathing example of strength, renewal and hope that people with a chronic illness have yet to see. I knew that my own experience of finding happiness, peace, and love within myself, even with a body part that had stopped working, would be a better inspiration than any Ted talk. Reflecting on the time in my life where I clearly had an imbalance in my body that led to my pancreas not working the way it should and developing into Type 1 diabetes, I could now see it from a bird's-eye view. Subconsciously, I held an underlying belief that I was not lovable. My own toolbox for surviving and thriving is in great achievement due to my own willingness to observe the deep learnings within myself and surrendering my life purpose to Universe.

I don't find it ironic that because of the way I grew up, with a feeling that something was missing (a father figure), that my pancreas was affected. Why? Because the pancreas is the part of the body that regulates glucose (sweetness) and plays a large part in our ability to make decisions. My mind had created my sickness—not the world, not Universe, but my ego, the "you haven't done enough" part of me that stayed a little too long in my consciousness, as a child. Universe gave me what I was missing: I lacked the sweetness of life, so I would *have* to eat sugar to function and stay alive. Carbohydrate counting was something I now *had* to do; carrying juice boxes was something I *had* to do, now. Universe knew that I needed to replace what wasn't working (quite literally) with happiness, joy and peace. Until I did this, I would hold onto the diabetes. Through seeing my life through the lens of lack and despair, I had invited myself to control something I didn't want! I knew it would take time, patience and my own willingness to reverse the old story of limiting beliefs I had told myself, in my younger years.

My rebirth was the undoing of what no longer served me; the limiting beliefs, the strongholds, and the "but, they said..." or "they told me so..." conversations I had heard and convinced myself of over the years. It was the release of what I had subconsciously learned and believed...until I "woke up." This gigantic shift in perception and developing a healthy, loving relationship with myself is what allows me to *be* well, *live* well, and move forward in my life! Establishing a daily practice of reprogramming my brain to *let go* of sickness so I could invite the healing power of the Universe to fill me was a *conscious* choice. I chose to surrender, and allow Universe to work in its perfect way, in its perfect time. This waiting...this trust...is what has led me to my most incredible days—YES! *Worth* living!

CHAPTER THIRTY-ONE

Forgive ... Forget ... Fulfillment

What if I were to tell you to forget everything you've ever learned? Maybe you'd wonder how starting again would be beneficial. To tell you the truth, I don't know anyone who has *all* the answers—such as, how to find a cure, why certain things happen, why some doors close and later, wider doors are opened. *No one* knows. But, what is meaningful is that by trying something new, we are *creating* new thought patterns, establishing new grooves in our brain, and having experiences from which our mind will learn.

Letting go of fear, the feelings of control, and judgment have led me to find purpose. Moving from a place of hardship to a place of recognizing that I *am* my own creation, and I *am* who I *believe* I am, has had the ability to heal and transform the quality of my life. As I am invited into this life as a co-creator of my own destiny, I understand that what I let go of will fall by the wayside, and what I invite *in* will stay, as long as I let it. This principle holds true for many of us who practice the art of *becoming*! I continue to stretch myself, in the way I relate to others, because I've learned to view my circumstances as *lessons* and my connections as *teachers*. These experiences have taught me, in an odd "I-don't-get-it-kind-of-way," how to love and accept who I am and who I present myself to be in this Universe. In time, I finally *did* get why certain lessons kept repeating themselves in my life: it wasn't until I learned them that I could move forward.

Take a moment to jot down some of the emotions that come up for you when you are uncomfortable so you can become aware of your "closed doors." What opportunities, people or feelings have fleeted you?

- Have similar relationships, opportunities or feelings come about since then?
- Who or what comes to mind?
- What effect has this had on your feelings about yourself or this person? Others?
- Where in your body do you feel it?
- How does it feel (stiff, cold, tight)?

Once you become aware of where this energy resides in your body, take a few deep breaths. Feel your breath move *through* your body as you envision a bright white light moving through the blockage and cleansing that area. Allow this feeling to penetrate your body while breathing in deeper and more steadily with each breath. Do this until you feel enveloped in this purifying light. Do this until the blockage seems to move harmoniously with the natural state and rhythm of your body. Congratulations! You're on your way to helping yourself heal!

CHAPTER THIRTY-TWO

'Scuse Me? Self-Care!

"You're always doing something. Ever since I've known you, you've always been that way—never sitting down, always working or finishing something," Meryl exclaimed. As mentioned in previous chapters, Meryl has been my best friend since about sixth grade, and she's incredibly good at telling it like it is. When I heard these words, I was meticulously placing each sock in my overstuffed sock drawer and trying to find the other magenta sock among the loosies. I was "sole-searching."

I thought about what Meryl said. "Wow, she's so right. I need to spend more time doing things that are playful and light, and that make me happy. Silence is great, to reflect...but, where do my passions lie?" I grinned, knowing that the Universe had guided her to bring attention to the fact that although I've become more attuned to myself and the power that lies within me, I was forgetting about an incredibly important part of life: *fun!*

In my mind, I thought about a professional development meeting we had in my school, a few weeks back. This meeting was led by a trained woman who enthusiastically tried to do her job and share her knowledge of wellness and self-care, though she seemed utterly stressed out. I couldn't help but laugh as she called upon me to "tell a little more about what you do." Later, a colleague made appreciative remarks about how *I* should be the one leading the class. I came to the conclusion that self-care is determined, scheduled, evaluated, and in every way completely dependent upon you, yourself. I say this because if you show up late for *yourself*, or you quit taking the time to care for *yourself*, it's likely that no one else will make mention or even notice. Luckily for me, my best friend helped point me toward a deep inner knowing and in the direction I knew I needed to go.

Within the last year, and after several "self-care" daily reminders in my cell phone, I have changed from being a diabetic feeling a loss of control, and loss of enthusiasm, to being a woman with an inconceivable amount of self-discipline. I have learned how to play the hand I was dealt, and play it well. I stopped overindulging on foods that made me feel good in the moment and quit numbing myself with obnoxiously loud music to rinse away the pain. Instead, I replaced these habits with more satisfying and fulfilling habits, such as singing, reading, stretching, or just finding the time to laugh or look up an interesting recipe. I observed that the Brittany I had become, and was living as, was not the one God had intended for me to be. I *knew* there was more for me! I came to recognize that I had been living more of an isolated life, than being one who was actually engaging in life. There was a whole world out there that I was ignoring out of fear and embarrassment of my diagnosis.

Being in my own head became too overwhelming. The doubtful conversations became too repetitive. The self-sabotage due to feeling a loss of control was too draining and uninteresting. I *wanted* to become a happier, better me. I wanted to become a stronger, healthier me. I decided then, to become a woman who was ready to grow and live up to my fullest potential. I would take Meryl's advice, and learn to appreciate the laughter, the love, and the blessings in my life. My recipe for healing? A dash of fun, hearty giggles, a *peace* mindset, and a whole lot of gratitude.

CHAPTER THIRTY-THREE

Becoming Unstuck

Taking care of yourself as a part of your own healing process takes dedication, diligence, and complete honesty. It takes time to become clear on what it is that you *really* want. What are your intentions? Think about them, meditate on them, draw a picture in your mind of what the healthiest, happiest, absolute best version of yourself would look like, act like, and feel like! I wish I could set up shop here and tell you that there is a finish line after becoming one with yourself. But, all there is is your *own* standard of progress to measure day in and day out—where you've been, where you are, and where you are going. I know—I've been there!

It takes willingness to stay steady and be forgiving, willing, and accepting. There may be moments in time where it feels hard to turn the mental chatter off. But, it is absolutely *necessary* if you want to live in peaceful harmony with *yourself*. Once you attain a desire to consciously build your inner self, you will soon start to crave the silence, the stillness that once seemed so unattainable. Boy, is it worth it to try—give it everything you've got! Consistently love yourself, and see how the world changes and adapts to your new beliefs about yourself! Your new perfect vision for your life will take root the moment you put these beliefs in the forefront of your mind.

As I started writing this book, it took every ounce of strength in me to revisit some very difficult times in my life. I was not forced, but rather guided, to share my experiences of loss, low self-esteem, and lack of love within myself and how I overcame defeat. As I mentioned in previous chapters, as a child, I was too young to recognize my own role in designing my life. The view I held of myself, believing all I *chose* to believe about myself inevitably put me on a path of conceiving a poor self-image, even as I matured. As an adult, I needed to become *accountable* for my choices. Acceptance and love, even with the hurts, the pain, and the disappointments are what eventually encouraged me to love myself even more. I loved myself the way Universe loves me, without the interference of my ego-driven mind. I chose unity over duality in my mind and in my life experience. I chose to love *myself*, above all—because without that, I could never appreciate anyone or anything else.

As Greek philosopher Heraclitus put it, "Change is the only constant in life." I remember hearing this quote as a little girl on the school bus. I would later think about this quote again, during the triumphs and setbacks of my self-created life. If the only constant *is* change, and God and our Universe are everlasting, ever-changing and ever-evolving, why then should we stop at one diagnosis and allow it to gather like sediment over our physical bodies, our emotional minds, and our spiritual gaze? We must recognize that the change we may so desire must always begin in ourselves, and in our cells.

Needless to say, my quest to curtail the widespread view of thinking that life beyond diagnosis is stagnant and unhealable was my primary focus. When I first had the idea of proactively beginning my healing journey, I was dabbling with basic principles of eating. I met with diabetes educators who told me to "eat one of those 100-calorie packs of Chips Ahoy" or "grab a candy bar" when I was having a low sugar episode. I've listened to fitness experts who told me to "exercise one hour on the Stairmaster per day, increasing up to two hours." They'd say to "take this supplement...cut that food group out...wear a waist trainer to melt belly fat..."— the list went on and on. Would anyone ever have success with any of these recommendations over the course of an entire life? No. Of course not, because bodies change, life circumstances change, environments change, *we* change! No method or checklist will work indefinitely, if it ever works at all.

My point is that I was told a *lot* of things about diabetes. And because my mind was so clouded with information from every person around me, I couldn't hear what *felt* right and real for my *own* body. It wasn't until years later that I appreciated that the only people I could trust were the doctors and other professionals with whom I had an established relationship—those who *truly* knew me and my history. My endocrinologist, Dr. Barry Schuval, was one of these very special people. He continues to advise me with love, care, and compassion. He cares for me as a human being, not just another body who showed up in his office every three months. I listened to his advice, his thoughts, and his plan of action, while also staying close to my *own* inner guidance. He supported me, and I supported him, and we continue to remain a team in regard to my proper diabetes care, treatment, and overall wellness.

In order to heal myself, I also quit rushing and placing unnecessary expectations on myself. When I became an Ayurvedic Nutritionist and Holistic Health Counselor, my teacher Dr. Naina would later confirm my own innate understanding; "no hurry, worry or curry!" meaning, no haste, no anxieties and no eating what is not good for your individual body constitution. I began by making small choices that would eventually make a *BIG* difference. I started off with eliminating the garbage that I had accumulated over all the years of my life—from toxic foods and chemicals, medications, sugar accumulation, and *sludge*.

I started re-introducing what my body knew best...nature's own foods with vitamins and nutrients from the *Earth*. Eating foods that were from the Earth helped me to become clear-minded and leveled—leaving behind the energies that were causing me to feel stuck. We'll call this installing a new energy filter. This filter released anything that didn't serve my body, my mind, or my life, any longer! A safe and methodical whole-food way of life sent a new invitation of life force energy to flow to every area of my mind and body, while eliminating the wastes that were ready to be evacuated. I began tossing out processed supplement bars and other packaged food I'd been using when I was on the go. To replace this habit, I made time in my schedule to plan my diet and eat intuitively according to what my body wanted, craved, and *needed*. I became a chef in my own kitchen, cooking up meals that I *knew* were safe, organic and healing for my body. Eating for health became my priority. Think: if it doesn't grow, don't eat it!

Disengaging from unhealthy activities, such as occupying spaces in my mind with comparison-type behavior and "should be" or "should have" self-dialogue, helped me turn the key in knowing and healing my *real* self. I ended judgment of myself and others, and I eliminated time spent on useless activities like scrolling through images of retouched, filtered, and enhanced photographs of people on social media. I realized that I had been allotting thoughts and energy to people in time and space that didn't *exist*. They had *no* place in the betterment of myself as a person, and they certainly weren't a positive stimulus helping me to see the beauty within *myself*. The two minutes here, three minutes there, forty seconds on this or that, scrolling, tapping, "liking," and searching did nothing to contribute to building the best version of myself—I was over it!

I disconnected from the meaningless, self-obsessed social media posters because what I needed to find wasn't on an app or social media feed—it was inside of *me*. I began spending more time in nature going for therapeutic walks, meditating, spending time with people I loved and who made me laugh. I also established a regular routine which I grew to love and enjoy... spending quality time with *myself*. These were the moments that brought me feelings of wholeness and happiness. These were times that empowered me to know and understand...*me!*

As I decluttered my cupboards, my closets, and even my "friends" list, my mind and my options for self-exploration became clear. I was creating space for growth, inspiration, and possibilities for myself! Finally, I became an instinctive vessel, acquiring a thirst for a healthier lifestyle. I was becoming a lighter and freer soul, as I gained insight into what freedom meant for me! This was made possible through my desire to become conscious of my subconscious mind. By empowering *myself* through changing my own routing system with my own manual updates.

CHAPTER THIRTY-FOUR

FOCUSED 'N' FREE

Meditation is a great tool that makes it possible to tune out all of the unnecessary noise and static around you. What I love about this practice is that within moments, you have the ability to *feel* like you're on a still, sandy beach with just the sound of the wind or a distant bird chirping in song. The moment is filled with quiet peace that immediately floods your heart center, wherever you are. Diabetes, for a long while, had me reminiscing about the days when I was "free." I don't think I even realized how much of my time was spent just existing in this body, re-enacting and living in memories of the past. In hindsight, yes, maybe I had been "free" of a diagnosis, but I wasn't *free* in my spirit. Now, when I look at my life, my situation has not changed, however; my *perspective* has. I may be living with a diagnosis, but I am more *free* than I have ever felt, due to my own involvement in learning and understanding myself. I believe that I have finally learned how to set myself free from my own self-imposed limitations.

When I started to connect with Universe and my inner self, I immediately began hearing and feeling wisdom that I'd never known. I like to ponder the biblical saying "We walk by faith, not by sight" because that is *exactly* what I learned to do. After investing more of myself in the trust I have in Universe and its plans for me, my life opened up to opportunities I never believed were possible. My faith and my trust were what inspired me to develop myself, fully, in my truth and rise as the woman I was meant to become.

When I turn back the pages of my life's lessons of feeling "attached" to my diabetes, but disconnected from life, I am reminded of the twists and turns that have gotten me here. Despite the challenges, I still find myself curious about where life will lead me. I listen to my inner voice and it's guidance, and by doing so, I am stretching myself and am able to reflect, learn and grow. I am able to acknowledge the events in my life that bring awareness to my being...those events in my life that subtly made me disengage from who I was. Doing so, gave me the ability to see myself not just as a body, but a soul, not just a human...but an *energetic being*. Not just as someone with a name, but someone with a *gift*.

The defeating comments and energies I had internalized are now disentangled and set free into the nothingness that they are: mere thoughts. I have chosen to release the undeserving thoughts that I had once held onto by recognizing them, detaching from them, and filling the void with what I like to call "Gratitude Thoughts." For example, thoughts such as, *"I am so thankful for the lessons I have learned. I am so grateful I am becoming all that I am meant to be. I am so appreciative of the pure love within me."* These types of thoughts can be expressed or meditated on to show appreciation for the lessons we have learned all along the way. It shows respect for ourselves and where we are at that point in our learning cycle. By replacing the old words with words of love and inspiration, the old thoughts dissipate back into the Light of the Universe. Forming loving, supportive thoughts will nurture the essence of the soul. Because of my own will to get to know these things I have told myself, it made me that much more able to recognize their influence in my life story, acknowledge them, and willingly let them go, so I may be set free.

Emerging as a new, healthier, happier me is quite a phenomenon, if you ask me! I was so attached to the person I once was...as it was all that I had known. It took time, practice, and repetition to release memories of those old stored moments, since I had held onto them for so long. Making a conscious effort to close the door to the parts of me that felt stuck and unmovable, I changed my belief system, my recurring thought patterns, and ultimately, my life. So much of what we *are* is our thoughts, memories, feelings, and core beliefs of ourselves. Our lives are so precious—I knew I could not withhold what has been so beneficial to my own healing—I wanted and needed to share it.

Realizing that it is in the most shadowed of times that we are challenged to seek and find the strength within, was what led me to believe in the possibility of becoming the woman that my younger self didn't know. I truly believe that we can evolve to the point of experiencing an extraordinary shift, leading to a more fulfilling, purposeful, and inspiring life. It *is* possible! It is when we set an intention to rely upon and trust this Higher Power, greater than ourselves, that we are able to experience freedom. This Higher Power is what sustains, provides, and orchestrates all of our interactions, connections, self-growth, discoveries, and strength. I came to deeply understand that this Power is in complete control of all time, space, and the soul's existence within the Universe—and therefore, us. We must respect *ourselves* so we may serve as a mirror for that same respect in our *world*.

Having an absent father growing up, I noticed my model for building healthy relationships with men was an aspect of my life that made me feel disconnected from love and from feeling a part of oneness in this Universe. Because I didn't have much communication with my dad and I grew up feeling unsure of where I stood with him, I had to learn how to *feel* comfortable with *receiving* a man's love. I knew this would be a primary focus for me: learning to become one with men and women alike—for there is no difference. Despite our physical differences, we were, are, and will always be one of the same. A part of my life work was recognizing this loving presence within myself and within *every* living thing.

With my father seldom around growing up, I adapted to who I felt I needed to be. I taught myself, subconsciously of course, how to keep myself busy during his frequent phone calls and how to compete with my brother for a chance to earn attention. I learned what I needed to do to fit his idea of who I should be. I don't fault my father, but his absence from my life was an obstacle I had to overcome. It was a learning experience that would teach a lesson in which I would need to learn in order to heal and be able to feel and express love as I entered adulthood. I learned through the inner dialogue and conversations with my Higher Self how to *be* the change I wished to see in myself. As a child, I didn't *understand* how to communicate, because what my brother and I had seen and heard was that one loves by leaving—or by not saying anything at all. However; this didn't mean that I couldn't learn how. Again, I practiced forgiveness. Clearly, my model for love needed to start within *myself* so that one day, I would show others how to love themselves, too.

My mother had an entirely different way of showing love: she was attentive, nurturing, supportive, and communicative. But, as a unit, the parenting model I saw and learned from made it tough for my brother and I to feel fully open to love and expression. We all did the best we could with the knowledge and experience we had. And that's all I, or anyone, can ask for. Unknowingly, I was entwined in a cycle of not understanding how to give love or receive it. Now, I have truly forgiven my father, because I recognize that he helped me to learn how to love myself and be a strong woman. His leaving I continue to forgive and send love to him, despite his choices of the past, because I now understand that the past really doesn't matter. He taught me the best skill I needed to survive in my life: how to love myself so I can create love in the world. I'd rather love him for that one special gift I had to learn, even in his absence.

I now know and believe that his leaving was never and will never be because of *me*. I've forgiven myself for all the things I told myself that *weren't true* as I was emerging in this body. Letting the past be the past allows me to be fully present in the most important and only time that matters: the now. This moment is where I am able to enjoy more of my beautiful, whole self, know my worth, and grow, as I live in harmony with the world. Give *yourself* the chance to re-learn, re-love and re-invite yourself back to your own life—the opportunity is *now!*

CHAPTER THIRTY-FIVE

Reprogram (for Your Own 'Gram!)

Have you ever said, or done, something quickly and then later kicked yourself in the derrière because you didn't mean to go there? Sometimes, we may feel defeated by our lack of progress because we've been letting our old, past ego and baggage come with us into our new experiences! A sure way to end this? Be *aware*—invite your conscious mind to be an observer of your subconscious mind. Watch your brain, and watch your thoughts—give yourself permission to reel it in when necessary!

The four-letter word that is often oh-so threatening and timorous—*fear*. Fear is like stuffing a big cotton swab in one ear and another in one's mouth—it suffocates one's purpose. Fear siphons off our ability to do what we are placed in this world to do. It can paralyze your ability to move, listen, grow, plan, and even think logically. When I started to become aware of the presence of fear in my life, both consciously and subconsciously, I made every effort to break through it. I began acting out of courage and deep faith, knowing that by living in fear, I was giving away my right to live *fully*. Deciding to give fear the boot and make a conscious effort to live *beyond* fear and into a movement of love, created space in my mind within which I could flourish.

I did this by acting with what felt right in my heart, at all times, without hesitation. I became well versed in recognizing that being uncomfortable is sometimes *necessary* because it helps us to learn more about ourselves and step out of complacency and therefore; boredom. I couldn't help but smile each time I thought of all the new seeds that I wanted to plant in myself. I knew I could do it—if there was a will, there most certainly would be a way!

The way to living a life on a foundation of love was to simply *reprogram*. Each of us has a system of thoughts and beliefs that have manifested into our physical experience of life. We are the way we are because of our conditioning. The best and only way to change your mindset, and your life, is through *re*-programming the program you *already* have installed. It's quite like a computer—you're updating your software. Fill your mind with affirmations and powerful thoughts that are most meaningful to you.

- What do you dream?
- What do you want to *feel*?
- How would your best self look?
- What would your best self act like?
- Who are you now versus *who you want to be*?

Surround your thoughts with positive energy, thoughts and feelings! Visualize where you foresee yourself! Step into the role of becoming a director, as you become clear on exactly what it is you want to experience in this life and who you want to present yourself to *be* in this world! Affirmations are one of my favorite daily self-care routines because they help me to remember *who I really am*. I also have observed how beneficial they are to my students. Creating affirmations, and reading and writing them every day, until you *believe* them, is a sure way to bring activity to the areas of the brain that may not be given the full credit they deserve.

Once the conscious mind becomes involved in the quiet mind (also known as the subconscious or observant mind), we can create harmony in which our thoughts, actions, and decisions are based solely on facts and truth, rather than on teetering emotions! Go ahead and write some down. Say them to yourself, have your children form them, even get your girlfriends in on it—share the power!

Here are some examples to get you started:

I *am* a beautiful human being.
I *am* full of great ideas. People love to listen to me!
I *am* healthy and strong!
I *am* always surrounded by people who love me and respect me.
I *am* creative!
I *am* worthy!

Now, you try it!

CHAPTER THIRTY-SIX

Sha-La-La-La-La ... Shifting

By now, you're probably curious about just exactly how I've started to feel better, live better, and laugh more. Maybe you're wondering how I've reclaimed my life and you're questioning whether you're strong enough to do it, too. If you would really like to know the most beneficial exercise and one of the best gifts you can give yourself, it's taking charge of your own mind.

If you've just been diagnosed with diabetes or another condition and haven't the first idea of how to help yourself heal, the advice that I am going to share is about what has helped *me* make life-changing efforts that have my doctors amazed and makes *me* feel like I have my life back! "This is unbelievable!" I've heard. "You've cut your numbers almost in half since your last visit!" "You're healthier than people without diabetes!" My answer? I've learned how to love, nurture and respect my soul. I've learned, through experience, how to live a life of true healing. If I can do it, I believe *you* can do it, too.

Now, I am focused on helping those of you who are genuinely ready to heal yourselves. OK! Glad you made it. You're ready! Or are you? You will have to prove it to yourself. So, your first homework assignment is to sit or stand in front of a mirror and introduce yourself. It may be uncomfortable or even somewhat weird, but I want you to look in the mirror and say, "My name is ___________ and I am making the decision to learn to love myself." Look right into your eyes and say it until you believe it. Do this multiple times a day as you walk past a mirror, your reflection in a window, hey, even if you're on the train. Pull out that mirror and spend some time loving *you*.

Great! You've taken the first step toward acknowledging that *you* matter! There is someone important inside that is ready to know *you*! Your involvement in this exercise recognizes the true essence of who you are—your *soul*! Through this mind–body connection, now comes the important stuff. We are going to be changing "I can't," "I won't," and "I don't have" into "I can," "I will," and "I have!" Using affirmative actions to declare our new, conscious state of being will be imperative to changing the old patterns and melting them away. Now, these are super powerful! The fantastic thing about affirmations is that *you* can design them to support what you would like to create in your life, no matter what your husband, wife, boyfriend, girlfriend, mother, brother, sister, friend, boss, or anyone else for that matter, thinks! This is a time to think about all the lovable qualities you have and all of the things *you* have dreamed of that you want to achieve.

Often, I begin by listing the beliefs I have about myself. So, for example, if you grew up in a family with one parent and struggled with feelings of being unloved, you may have inadvertently taken on the soul concept "I am not lovable." If this belief is no longer serving you (of course, it never did, and never was true), then we are going to make a mental shift in this belief toward a real-life affirmative declaration: "I am *so* lovable." Say it! Shout it! Make it clear! *Oof! That feels good!* You can use the table below as an example to help you analyze some of your own self-created beliefs and change them into positive, affirmative present-time beliefs. Even if you don't believe them now, you *will* once you begin to train your mind, so it is very important to write these phrases in the present tense.

OLD LIMITING BELIEFS	NEW BELIEFS
I am unworthy.	I AM so worthy of love!
It is hard to be loved.	It is easy for me to attract love from the right people into my life at exactly the right time.
I am not smart enough.	I AM incredibly wise. I am always learning and excelling at what I do.
I am not enough.	I AM more than enough! Everything I need is always on its way to me, in perfect time.
I am not attractive enough.	I AM beautiful on the inside and the outside!
I never get recognition for my hard work.	I AM receiving recognition for my amazing work ethic.

Now that you see how to turn your negative, hindering thoughts into constructive, positive beliefs about yourself, choose a couple to say to yourself each morning in the mirror. Say them as you drive, as you're hailing a cab, as you're chillin' your heels in a waiting room, or even as you wash your hands before lunch. Make saying these statements a steadfast routine, wherever you are, at whatever time you can. Say them, sing them, write them, type them—however you do it, make these beliefs your blueprint for starting your new life and refashioning your self-image! *You've* got this, and you're *worth* the time and effort these simple little sentences require—they will change your life for the better! Speak your truth and *believe* in your truth. Express it consistently with a big smile on your face. Your future self will thank you!

CHAPTER THIRTY-SEVEN

Finding the Courage to Become Visible

Mustering the courage to leave behind what *wasn't* working for me was challenging. I had to decide how I wanted my life to flow, stick with it, and steadily exercise and live it in my daily life. I knew I had a message to share, but how would I do it? I realized that I had to learn what *wasn't* working so that I could choose a new path that *did* work. I had to leave behind the old patterns that didn't serve me so I could create new patterns that *would*. Planning my new life, building relationships that were valuable (especially the one I had with myself), and changing my attitude about the circumstances and events in my life was key to my growth. Being receptive to change, in order to evolve and become the best version of myself, was another major choice... but I was ready, so the work I chose to put in, was worth *it*.

I'll admit it—it took *time* for me to choose the path of resistance, one that was so different from the one I had commonly tried, the path of *least* resistance. But eventually, I became bored with the old stories I told myself and my tiresome thoughts. Still, my ego tried to make an appearance. "No one cares. You probably have nothing to say that someone else hasn't already said. There's already about 12.5K Instagrammers and bloggers reaching this population of people, Brittany—give it up. Your ideas aren't going to get you anywhere unless you're half naked on a live stream for everyone to follow—*then* you'd be 'likable' or 'a success.'" I tackled each ego comment one by one, redirecting it to my positive, affirmative thought. Then, I smiled and waited, knowing I was getting better and better at ignoring my fearful, ego-driven mind.

I heard the voice that I've heard repeatedly since I was a little girl, telling me to share who I am—to share my story—but, I wasn't sure how. I knew where I was, and I knew the life I was currently living, but I didn't have all the answers I felt I needed to have—the conclusion. I caught fear in its tracks and my 365-days-a-year secretary was working overtime, beeping in to remind me of what I was here for. I convinced myself I should wait...just keep waiting. But, I knew that wasn't the answer. "This is okay," I convinced myself, "...because I'm still in the ebb and flow of life, discovering who I am." I started thinking...and thinking. I came to realize that I really didn't know *anyone* who knew their absolute final destination, right here, right now. I gathered that maybe that's intentional—we're not meant to *know*...because if we did, our faith would be underdeveloped, and our creativity and exploration would be minimized, since we would "know it all."

While listening to a podcast that I just happened to stumble on, I tapped into myself and found a new thought: I needed to invite myself to become visible. Not sure of what this message meant, I spent a few moments in stillness waiting for what Universe wanted me to understand. What I needed to do, if I wanted to create positive and lasting change, was to leave behind habits and thoughts that I had accumulated, unknowingly and unwillingly. There was *still* an unsettled part of me that was still holding on to all that I had known. I took this as a learning curve and started devoting more time to my affirmative and mindful practice.

I knew the answers were deep inside of myself, as I sought to unveil my soul. The only way I could learn about my soul was by paying close attention to the things that I was passionate about (what felt like "home") and the things that made me want to flee. These triggers would tell me the areas in my life that I needed to pay attention to.

To become visible, I had to invite myself, for starters, to *love* who I am. Because I *am* special, and I *am* one of a kind. I said it until I *believed* it. There is no one in this world with the same DNA and character traits as mine...that's *why* I'm worthy of knowing, loving, respecting, and valuing myself! "I *am* funny, I *am* wise, I *am* upbeat, I *am* creative," I affirmed. I stared at myself in the mirror telling myself what is true, despite the initial urge to try and resist it. In time, I grew to finally hear my own living truth and I began to believe the words coming out of my mouth. As I set challenges for myself each week and noticed my thoughts, feelings, and behaviors toward myself, I knew that what I was doing was working. I changed the tune of my track again, pressing forward, and persisting in the new direction I had created for my life. I felt myself coming into a deeper sense of the woman I always knew myself to be. I am confident that *you* have a set of gifts inside of yourself, too! What about yourself makes you unique? Think about the qualities you have that make *you* lovable and *worth* knowing! This is your time to showcase your best attributes, *express* them, and bring them into your life!

When I made the choice to become visible—to be courageous, to be powerful, to share who I *really* am, inside and out—my world started to blossom. This simple shift in consciousness opened up the gateways to opportunities that I saw myself able to achieve. To heal, we must be open and receptive to *all* of our utmost positive qualities that we have to present in this world. Think about the compliments, the awards, the surprises and milestones you've reached in your life that maybe don't tell you, but *show* you, that you *are* worthy of recognition and love! Only when you make the conscious decision to embrace the beautiful human being that you already *are* will you accept and welcome love into the areas of your body, and your life, that need it most. Only then, will you be able to help yourself and inspire others to do the same. You will be creating and living in alignment with the law of Universal Oneness.

Whatever your belief system, your background, or your unique knowingness, it is my honest and sincere belief that we are all here because of the great I AM Presence of the Universe. I believe it was our *choice* to be brought into existence in human form to learn what we hadn't learned about ourselves before—to continue to search and seek the light of the soul that lies within each of us. That is why we have our life's work cut out for us! The aspects of life that seem most irritating, frustrating, or difficult, give us clues about the parts of our soul that are unhealed, and direct us to turn *within ourselves* to discover our deepest truth. For example, if you find yourself continually seeking respect from others, but they keep letting you down, there is a high probability that your consciousness doesn't truly *believe* that you are worthy of respect. Until you respect *yourself* and *your* core truth, you will be faced with experiences that mirror this underlying belief.

Oh! The movements, relationships, growth opportunities, lulls, and excitements of life! We are, in essence, created to survive and learn from our past. Our purpose is evolution and learning how to stand back up after being tumbled down. Our mind is the most important tool we have because it is what enables us to experience our living reality. It is a tool that allows us, through our own connection with Source, to control what we see through our mental images, our self-talk, and our core beliefs.

Our mind challenges us to bring to the forefront what we have learned about ourselves, our choices, and our experiences. Then, we can create new pathways to achieving our highest good and sharing that goodness with the world. Our past was created by a subconscious inability to control our thoughts. Most of us mirrored what we saw, mimicked what we heard, and replicated what was within our reach—family patterns, friendships, relationships—only to find later, that these patterns may not serve us as we seek to move forward in a more satisfying and fulfilling way. This is where the self-work comes in! Knowing better, and loving yourself, still, will keep you mindful of the right actions to take in learning and living the life you've always dreamed of!

Many of us live our lives with the repetitious mannerisms and conduct that our ego likes to be in control of in order to benefit itself. However, when you listen to that inner voice inside you (that we all are fully able to tap into at any given moment), you may find that you can be divinely guided by that deep inner voice. It is our inner knowing that comes alive and empowers us to make decisions that seem most fitting for us, on our own individual missions. The more that you welcome, respect, and appreciate your inner voice, the more confident you will feel about becoming accountable for the parts of yourself that you want and are willing to change. It is all a matter of choosing the right voice—your own, the voice that speaks to us and calls out to us when we may least expect it, but need it!

This voice, (that you may try to tune out) can serve as your best friend, your best ally, your brightest light because it speaks *wisdom*. It is your deep knowingness, your intuition, your center. If you want to receive joy, you must *be* joy for others. If you want to *be* cared for, you must care for others. We must recognize that we cannot receive what we do not give. When you choose to give not only to yourself, but to others, you will see your life start to open as you form your own unique relationship with your Higher Self and with Source, guiding you to follow your own true calling. Soon, you will feel a direct shift in the way the Light is shared with you to bring forth your true essence, happiness, and love within all of your soul and all of your surroundings.

CHAPTER THIRTY-EIGHT

VROOM ...VROOM ...VISUALIZE!

As spoken about in earlier chapters, if we don't take responsibility for *deciding* who we are, then we will unknowingly learn to live up to what the people around us say and do to tell us who we are! That seems like an awfully big expectation. But, it's too *easy* to push away the work that we must do on *ourselves*. It can be *so* much easier to just be who and what people tell us to be. I like to think that it is the most admirable and brilliant minds that are *brave* enough, and *willing* enough, to break that mold. I found myself thinking: how can I share my love and past struggles to create profound change? I practiced becoming responsible for my own life and made choices based on what I wanted to experience.

I started to think of the way girls are taught from the minute we exit the womb: constantly playing house with our make-believe family—pretending to feed them, brush their hair, change their clothes—all before we're even in nursery school. We've *learned* to give ourselves away to care for the dolls—correction, the world around us. *Take care of ourselves? What does that mean?* We become what we have seen, time and time again, stemming from our grandparents, our parents, and our society.

The virtual tunnel of perfectionism and escapism through the glass screen of our technological devices has become too normal, for too many. It's no wonder the number of women with eating disorders has increased out of proportion. There are more nine-year-old girls walking around, dressed like fashion models or social media "idols," self-obsessed about their own superficial appearances, rather than how to make an actual difference in the world. A shift in our own consciousness will help us to see, respect, and honor what is right in front of our eyes, right here, right *now*. A shift that would awaken our own deep knowingness to create a movement of believing in our own inner radiance, that there is no need to give ourselves away. Not to *anyone*—not to *anything!*

We tend to believe that our circumstances and feelings are permanent. Instead of accepting that illusion, why not capture each moment in time and express ourselves as we are in that very moment? What about stepping outside ourselves and our egotistical ways and focusing on what's really meaningful? What about investing the time that we spend comparing ourselves to others, and reorganizing that to time to better match our own selves? What if we made the conscious shift to become involved in enhancing our *own* perceptions through our very own self-talk, reflection and growth? Giving up control is the first step to achieving freedom. It all begins with this desire; the one powerful choice to simply surrender to what *is*.

CHAPTER THIRTY-NINE

Food as My Witness

Through my willingness to surrender, I noticed that I started to grow comfortably into myself. I began to navigate my inner being and find my own inner peace, even in the long bumper-to-bumper drives to the public school I worked at in Jamaica, New York. I knew that I was sent to do work in a community that needed my love and support.

After a full day of teaching for eight hours each day, I couldn't help but think about why I had been placed around kids in an impoverished area with broken families, distrust, and poverty. It was that still time between changing lights that allowed me to reflect on the guidance I was receiving from above. It became clear to me that I was meant to be there for these children, who didn't have very much, so I could teach them to believe in themselves. These children never knew if they would have a hot meal when they got home or if they would be seeing their imprisoned dad anytime soon, but they still managed to show up cheerful, ready, and engaged. Maybe God had a way for *me* to learn something from these kids. Maybe it isn't about what we have, had, will have or won't have, can't have, or might not have enough of. It made me consider that maybe we each *already* have *exactly* what we are supposed to have. I found myself listening and observing the dialogue Universe was having with me in the stillness of my mind. My inner conversations led me to believe that I had come to a moment in my life when it was time to move onward and upward. It was time for me to begin priming my wings to fly in a new direction, stretch myself, and give back to the Universe in a larger way.

I can't say there was any one moment that changed the way I saw my life. Rather, I had several ongoing, continuous conversations with God as I strived to get out of my own head and gain insight about my next steps toward living my life as the woman I had always dreamed I would be. I waited for a sign, a conversation, or the right person to come along and guide me to gain insight into what I needed, to find my own answers. I didn't seek an absolute "yes" or a "no" from anyone or anything. But, I did *pay attention* to what I *heard*, what I *saw*, what I *felt*, and what I *knew*. I trusted myself, and knew that if I stuck with this commitment to following my truth, I would soar, because I was *ready* to. I can say earnestly that it is all my interactions, both planned and unplanned, that have made me who I am today—physically, emotionally, and spiritually. You'll see what I mean as I share how we all are students in this thing called life!

CHAPTER FORTY

Here to Hear

I've often pondered the importance and relevance of making mistakes. Maybe the "whoops!" and "I'll do it better next time" opportunities are life's way of showing us the parts of ourselves that we must pay closer attention to. Maybe the mistakes are our teachers, our lessons, our necessary check-ins with ourselves, to ensure that we learn *what we came here to learn*. Maybe the times of frustration, transition and setback are Divine opportunities for Universe to guide and support us in our life journey, speaking or not speaking to us so we may better hear *ourselves*. Sometimes the events in our lives serve as a big, red symbolic stop sign, which are used to slow us down, protect our *spirit,* and preserve who we truly are.

"Time heals all wounds." We've all heard it, but do we *believe* it? If you are willing to let go of the past and feel ready to step into your brightest future, you may find this statement will reveal its truth. Reflecting on my own accomplishments, challenges, relationships, friendships, travels, and experiences I've had, I am amazed by my inner growth. I am still the same soul who has not only outlived, but became stronger from all of these things I couldn't imagine doing, then.

In my journey of self-discovery, I became interested in healing myself using self-analysis and several holistic, alternative approaches to restore my mind–body balance and through connecting to the vital energy of the Universe. I am fortunate to have discovered and learned of the true beauty within myself and my world, even with pricking my finger and squeezing blood several times a day. If I can do it, I *know* you can, too!

Maybe it was boredom from *watching* my life instead of *living* my life, or maybe it was those extra breaths I took to soothe the anxiety I felt from the constant chatter in my mind...but, whatever it was, there was a time and space for me to come to recognize my *own* self-worth. I grew uninterested in comparison-type living and the attachments to the fantasy life that was presented through the glass screen of my cell phone. Finally, I checked in with *myself*. "Lazy morning! I woke up like this" (with eyeliner, lashes, fresh curls, lip gloss on fleek, and prop settings)—no, thank you. I finally realized *my* truth outside a digital realm of illusion and egotism. I learned to enjoy life with the woman that I *am*.

Finally, I came to the point where the person that I most needed to take care of, was *me!* By reclaiming the relationship with myself...I naturally came into alignment with my own truth, and the relationships and opportunities that suit me best! Making time to enjoy my *self*, the core being of who I am, is what has given me the power to accomplish all that I dream. It invites me to see the gifts of life—in all things—and flow with the rhythm of life, rather than fight it.

Seeking alternatives to help me feel well, I sought out acupuncture. As my treatments became a regular part of my weekly health regime, I knew it would take time to resolve the unsettling feelings caused by years of allowing sugar into my blood and cells. Numerous times, as I lay on the table with needles inserted into my skin, I could sense the tingling of emotions that would surface and release into tears, while grasping the edge of the table.

A cheery woman named Andrea would sit at the foot of my bed and keep me company when I felt uneasy. At times, being alone with myself in a dark room with needles in my body did just that. Andrea would comfort me and remind me, "It's okay! Your body is accepting the healing. Just breathe, Brittany; you're not breathing. Allow the healing to take place. I am here for you." I felt tears drip down my cheeks, not because I was sad, but because I was releasing old emotions that were leaving my physical body. She wiped my tears and held my hand. I was amazed with the release that came, time and time again. Years of my old self being shed, melting away into the table that supported me. She reminded me to "just let it go." And finally, *I did.*

Sprawled out on the cold table, I prayed for the pure, loving energy of the Universe to flow through me. I had nothing to grasp onto or cling to but my faith. An array of emotions, peace, and love filled my body as I drifted into a deep state of rest. Yearning for the feeling of being free again, I counted..."inhale 1...2...3...4... hold breath...exhale...5...6...7...8..." I watched my chest expand, rising high and filling with such anticipation and anxiety, then collapse, as I let go and released all the scattered thoughts of my mind. The feelings I experienced were otherworldly—and I felt immediate liberation and tranquility. I invited my eyes to flutter open and shut while feeling the sweat of my palms receive the Chi (energy) from the needles, bringing healing and balance into my body.

As I released what I had worked my whole life to hold onto, I was taught a *new* way—to let go and let God in. I wanted *so* much to know myself better. I welcomed every possibility for living a larger life, with purpose, and developing the consciousness that would help shape me into the woman I was created to be. I didn't want to be the Brittany *I* had chosen to design and create in my own self-righteous way—she was too lonely, too fearful. I chose to have the way of God over my own ways.

I sent a new invitation out that carried inspiring thoughts, intentions, and desires, to God and to myself. I asked for forgiveness of my sins and for Him to help me forgive myself for my past failures. My vision was clear, and properly and purposefully prepared, with love and trust behind it. I was ready to be involved in my own healing journey and experience the full life that God ordained for me. I knew it was there and that it had been there all along—but I was too disconnected to see it. Tapping into Source, I found the strength within myself to continue on. Acting on my new vision and desires, I trusted that a daily dose of mindfulness would surely get me there, with perfect timing.

CHAPTER FORTY-ONE

Raising the Bar and Rising Up

It was Deepak Chopra who once said, "There are no extra pieces in the Universe. Everyone is here because he or she has a place to fill, and every piece must fit itself into the big jigsaw puzzle." Feeling like one of the pieces of a puzzle, I dove headfirst into my third bodybuilding competition, a whole lot wiser than the first-time Brittany of years earlier. After becoming more aware of myself through my meditation practice and a solid period of self-love and self-care, I felt ready to re-emerge as a healthier, happier, and more accepting Brittany than I had *ever* been.

However; this time around, I chose to do things quite differently. This time, I gave up the expensive rhinestone bikini and taught myself how to jewel my own. I went from over four coats of tanning to a mere two, and instead of the typical pillow stuffing for my breasts, I wore my own. I told *no one* I was doing it. I was doing this for myself. Raising the bar for myself. Elevating the standards I held for myself and the vision I had for my life. I was clear that this time around, it wasn't just about being physically strong, but *mentally* strong. This wasn't about a ranking. It was about finally finding, respecting, and honoring myself for all that I was and all that I *am*.

Years had passed and I was now at a place in my life where I wanted to make up for lost time, especially after hiding myself for so many years. I was proud to be a woman who wore her diagnosis as a badge of honor. I knew I deserved that, after all the hard work I had done on myself. The healing was happening... and I *knew* it! But, I knew I needed to stay steadfast in my faith to continue on and finish what I had started.

The day was long as I arrived at the show with a suitcase of necessities to last me through the day. Rice cakes, sweet potatoes, glucose tabs, my journal and a good read to keep my mind occupied—I knew where my energy and my attention needed to be. I watched and yawned as I gazed out toward the stage. "BIKINI CLASS! Head on backstage!" I found my way through the crowds of sweaty tanned men and women just trying to find a seat on the floor and surpass the oil-slabbing and resistance band pumping. I found a spot on a grungy towel, soiled with self-tanner imprints and coconut scented balm, next to a young woman named Cassandra. She had just come back from the military and we shared our triumphs and trials through the preparation just to get here. I found comfort in her life story, listening to her own discovery of inner strength, too.

Eight o'clock in the morning soon became 3 p.m. and at last, it was time for the bikini class to go live. We lined up as a group and headed toward the curtain, many nervously smiling at one another. I noticed something different! I felt secure...trusting... giddy...and at peace. I guess you could say I did a pretty epic job of maintaining my peace and upholding my power. *Intelligence* told me this was a competition, but *wisdom* taught me the competition was within myself, and defeating my old, undeserving patterns. No one else, nor the number of hours they spent looking in the mirror at themselves, would have any gauge on how *I* presented myself and ran my own race that day. I took note of each person whose body turned more and more green as their sweat mixed with the chemicals of the tanning solution, leaving them with quite the look to bring on stage. I found myself laughing as each *still* sized up one another, clearly convinced of how "hot" they looked. Uninterested by the big headedness, I found myself looking at the clock.

I approached the stage taking one big final breath and walked casually and confidently to the center of the stage. I walked where I felt guided to go, smiled at who I wanted to smile, and took my time being conscious of where I was in that moment. I twisted, I twirled, I swayed, until finally...*I did it!* I *did it* as a complete, healthy, solid, confident young woman who *already* knew her worth. I clapped and stood with the bright lights shining on my face, as the rest of the competitors came out. I can honestly say I felt sorry for some of these girls who put all of their pride and self-esteem in someone else's hands—as I had once made that mistake and been there once before, too. Sure, I had my medical device on, and my abs may have had a different showcasing than the others...but, what did that matter? What I wanted everyone to see was my willingness, inner strength and resilience to still arrive at the final destination. Absolutely *zero* hesitation, doubt, or shame in my package! When the final call outs were called, my number wasn't...but, somehow I knew that meant nothing now. I knew that #9 was still #1, as my Higher Self had already been called *forward*. That was much more important to me at this phase of my life. I knew it was my time to recognize that being a winner doesn't mean going home with a trophy. It doesn't even mean other people need to see what I tried so hard all my life to prove. I proved myself, *to* myself and this victory was one I waited for all my life.

I jumped and walked speedily to the edge of the stage. My smile was brighter than any camera could have captured that night, as I felt a sense of peace overwhelm every cell in my body like never before. I clapped and kicked off my high heels, tore off my fake lashes and shouted *"YES!!!"* scurrying across the floor *without* my five-inch stilettos. Despite what the audience may have thought or not thought, I knew that 9th place was the perfect place to be. Because inside...I knew I had already won my biggest challenge...loving myself, every day, no matter *what!* I checked all the boxes on my own scorecard. Winners one through eight may have had a little extra applause that night for the physical appearance that made them appear to have "wanted it more" but, what *I* wanted was my own recognition of my true self...and this girl *got it*! It didn't matter what anyone else thought! I had won a victory in myself from the core of my being—I made *my own* call out. My own, *FINAL* call out—Brittany Hines, a *masterpiece,* had been found and was here to stay! I drove home with clear confirmation and a deep sense of acknowledgment that night. I finally identified with the beautiful woman I always was, I saw her...loved her...and invited her to stay.

CHAPTER FORTY-TWO

Coming Back to Life

There are many moments in our lives that, whether we like it or not, mold our design inside and out. It may be hard to comprehend and accept that every conversation, every encounter, every pat on the back, and even every criticism or heartbreak, has the potential to shape our human mosaic. Our every experience creates a thought. That thought is felt and carried with us all throughout our life in the way we look, think, act, and speak. It is up to us to choose whether to hold onto these thoughts or, at a certain point in time, realize they are no longer serving us and release them.

When I was pre-diabetic, emerging into young adulthood, I decided I wanted to get rid of my straight hair by perming it. I wanted thin eyebrows instead of my full natural brows. As a matter of fact, hand me the tweezer, let's rip them all out! I bought jeans that were too tight and shirts that were too short. I *enjoyed* who I was designing myself to be because I did what I wanted, without hesitation or fear of what the world might think. What Brittany felt like doing, wearing, or thinking, that's what she did. I felt so comfortable making my own decisions without fear of judgment and just freaking *rocking* it!

It was when I started unintentionally letting others determine who I should be that I lost my antenna for becoming myself and living my truth. Recognizing this was my immediate first step to taking my own power *back*! My rainbow popsicle would melt, and my self-esteem would hit rock bottom. When it came time to reveal the real me, I felt that I needed to hide. I realized that I wasn't giving *myself* the respect, the time, or the love that I needed to survive. In hindsight, I realize that I had *no* idea who I was, despite thinking I did. I was travelling along, on a one-way street, on the journey of my life, until my big "U-Haul truck moment" came along to pick me up and *redirect* me.

My own "U-Haul truck moment" was when I ended up in the hospital and was diagnosed with Type 1 diabetes. This moment arrived at an unexpected time, in an unexpected place, with no scheduled pick-up or drop-off date, and it carried me into action, direction, and self-exploration. One way I like to think of it is that God had me tune into the radio station of my life by listening to His words and allowing me the experience of this channel. He helped me turn the knob, to tune in and turn on, to hear the messages I needed to hear. Through the twists and turns of my life, I was guided to become an experiencer of life rather than a floater, or observer of life. After the jolt of having to learn how to manage the diabetes and live my life on insulin, I slowly began living *fully* by visiting and revisiting the young woman I was in the mirror. I began to enjoy getting to know myself in a *whole* new way. I made room for me to grow and learn from my past experiences.

I decided to schedule myself into the appointment that is my life, show up as the main event in my *own* life! I figured it was best to be involved and *love* who I am. Symbolically, I began piling one box after another into the U-Haul truck. Each box held old thoughts, energies, objects, and patterns that needed to be discarded. And in discarding them, I rediscovered space within my mind, my body, my world, and most importantly, my route to discover God. No glossy magazine or monthly "how-to" tips would teach me about the most valuable gift in my life—my connection to my Higher Self. I felt clear and focused knowing I was not alone. I also knew that we all can access this divine connection because it exists in each and every one of us. Despite not having all the answers right at my fingertips, I began making small changes through shifts in my thinking patterns, to fill the now-open space with new, healing and purposeful thoughts! Soon, I began to see positive changes in my life and—I wasn't afraid to dream. I wasn't afraid to live. I wasn't afraid to emerge as the woman God created me to be!

CHAPTER FORTY-THREE

Doing a U-Turn Back onto Consistent Lane

Doing is what directly creates our life experience. I like to think that I'm a doer. I think every human likes to "*do*." That means different things for everyone—a baker, a teacher, a doctor, a salesperson, a student, or a mother, but we all like to "*do*." We like to think, in our self-created state of mind when we wake up each day, that we will be productive and engage in activities and conversations that will lead to a sense of well-being or satisfaction. As we *do* things, it is important to ask ourselves in the moment: am I happy? Content? Present in thought? Anxious? It's all a frame of mind created by our ability to handle not only our physical actions, but our mental ones, as well. This is the reason some people feel tired or drained, even without any medical issues—for too long, their inner selves have been ignored.

When we listen to what our soul wants, we tend to make choices—about people, activities, jobs—that reflect our inner state of consciousness, bringing us to experience a greater sense of peace. We gain a sense of feeling that in the moment, *all* is well. We create a window of opportunity that provides us with a feeling of space and deep knowingness, no matter where we are, because we are making choices that are *in alignment* with what makes our soul happy.

When I reflect back on myself, what I wanted was to see *new* things! I guess in a way, I chose to do nothing—to procrastinate, so I could be "still." Maybe I was just content not knowing anything different and holding on to what I knew at that time. I focused on what I *thought* would make me happy by trying new things, buying new clothes, meeting new people or having new experiences, only to discover that these ideas did not bring *lasting* happiness. Everything I wanted, or I thought I wanted, was to benefit myself. It was my ego's way of trying to control and find happiness *outside* of who I was.

The stillness I sought could only be experienced if I would embrace the challenge of opening myself up to the opportunity of deep inner healing through digging into the depths of my soul. Knowing this, I did everything I could to change my old established habits that weren't working and create new pathways for myself to experience. My greatest teacher has been facing my own shadows and learning through my own lessons. What I needed to recognize was not necessarily the *new* things—but the things that have been there all along, but I was too preoccupied to see. What I understand now is that I had to re-learn the world as I knew it—not changing what I saw, but changing *how* I saw. Going *within* was the only way "out."

Thank God for my "healthy" medical reports, it was like I relearned what I *thought* I had already figured out—the art of being happy. An immense sense of peace became obtainable the *minute* I put my attention on building my inner world, instead of my outer world. I knew that this healing was only made possible through God. I also knew that it took my part to listen to His guidance. I give boundless thanks and gratitude for my meditation practice, lifestyle and diet changes, hands-on healing, being in tune with my mind, my body, my thoughts, my feelings, and of course, my endocrinologist! The lesson here—and it has appeared and reappeared until I finally got it—is that no person, place, or thing will ever have the ability to make me, or anyone else, happy. That is, until we are willing to truly see ourselves in a vision of love, and fix the parts of ourselves we are meant to heal. I came to an understanding that happiness and healing are made possible *from within.* I had to rediscover my true self and get to a point where I cared about *myself* before I could let the world mirror that same love and care to me.

What I learned from having this life-changing diagnosis was that what I *thought* I wanted, didn't really benefit my soul. Getting what *I* wanted didn't lead me to any more happiness than I had experienced the day before. It was the routine and not knowing any better that kept me stuck in the monotony. I didn't believe that *I* could change anything. It was as though I accepted that life happened to me as a passenger, instead of being the driver in control. "Just believe," I would always hear, and I kept thinking, "Would God or Universe even want to hear from me?" The crevices of my mind were filled with despair and lack of direction. Becoming fully aware of this, I knew I felt ready to face the fears that held me back. I discovered my own path through my own initiative to better understand and know myself through the power of Oneness.

Leaving the hospital on the night of March 11, 2008 with a shattered heart, a pile of medical papers and a pocket-sized carbohydrate counting book, I felt so alone, uncertain and lost. I felt as if my plan to become all that I was meant to be had hit a major fork in the road. I struggled for a very long time with my self-image and with feeling good about myself. I struggled with connecting to others. I struggled with loving myself. I struggled with feeling deserving. Surely, I was meant for more...but, I couldn't help but wonder how I would get there, and when?

In my growing desire to ask questions and pay attention to the signs and experiences around me, day after day, month after month, and year after year, I realized that God had used this one pivotal experience in my life to direct my attention toward Him. It was through that disappointing, dark, hollow event in my life that I was guided to discover myself, and my worth, one day at a time. I was asked to rise higher and to know God. As I worked meticulously, traveling on the path of my own healing, I stayed in constant communication with my inner soul through monitoring my daily thoughts, emotions, energy and feelings. Whether it was adjusting and tailoring my own diet changes to match what my body needed, or incorporating pranayama, yoga, salt baths, or simply buying myself some flowers at Best Market, I sought to find and *develop* my happiness.

My pursuit to find what the ashrams, the yoga studio, the "Quiet Room," or the sacred space offered, led me to set aside time to be alone with myself and connect to my Highest Power. I wanted to understand myself, my soul, and my mind. I wanted this for myself because I knew that I would be able to master the art of happy living by putting in the work that no one else could do for me. I would learn the most *about* myself, *for* myself, to *free* myself and understand my true purpose of why I am *here*. I walked this path not just for my own well-being, but for those around me who also were ready to discover the way out of their self-created labyrinth and into their true essence, expressing themselves fully, with their inner Light!

In my quiet time, I made daily reflections, speaking aloud or journaling to express my ideas, thoughts, and understandings to Universe. It was through this expression of energy that I was able to free myself of guilt, anger, and dismay. This letting go is what ultimately brought me closer to the insights and infinite love of the Universe. This was when I opened the door to welcome myself with open arms and experience my true spiritual awakening. I spoke, I wrote, I cried, I sang, I danced, I thought, I reflected, I listened, I watched...and I waited. And I waited, more...until finally, I recognized the power in the wait as being one of the most healing, regenerative, restoring aspects of this entire healing journey. I appreciated the experience of being fully present in my human existence, to watch and feel myself re-emerge as a more alive woman than I had ever been!

CHAPTER FORTY-FOUR

The Meditative Movement

So, how can you re-emerge as *your* best self? Start by meditating on what it is that you would like to see of yourself, for yourself. Imagine peace washing over you from above, cleansing you from prior beliefs. Clean the slate and be open to a new pathway. Then, think about all that you would like to be, all that you would like to accomplish, and all that makes your inner light shine. You know yourself best! What makes you happy? Next, begin reflecting on your life experience. Think of your younger self from birth up to your current stage in life. Ask yourself the following questions:

- What was your family life like?
- What was your social life like?
- What significant events do you remember?
- What moments in time are memorable to you?

Take some time to jot down some specific moments that you remember, both positive and negative. Throughout each phase that you revisit in your mind, allow your thoughts to come and go. Try to zoom into the events that come up for you naturally. The thoughts or memories that arise most naturally tend to be the thoughts or beliefs you may have been holding onto, subconsciously, of course, to create the person you are currently living as, and are experiencing.

Focusing on the events that happened in the earlier parts of your life are key to understanding the person you have become, because these are the events that are most established in your mind! Once you have had some time to journal these events and think about the role these events have had on your character or personality throughout your life then, start to piece together the information that guides you to know when *you* feel you may have handed in your own "exit slip" to who you truly are. When did you maybe throw in your own towel, a bit too soon? Think of these events as little pebbles that over time creates one large, hard rock. Acknowledging when you may have unintendedly or subconsciously left the whole person you once were, will help you to piece together the parts of yourself you may like to bring healing to, now.

Revisiting these memories in your mental files is critical to understanding the personality traits, conditions, and thoughts you subconsciously created because of your surroundings and early relationships with others. They may be considered a paper trail, which will lead you to discover at what age, in time and space, you made the subconscious decision to separate from the person you truly are inside and from all that you were intended to be. The next step to discovering your authentic self is to distinguish the subconscious mind from the conscious mind. How? Close your eyes and take a mental walk through your memories. When you open your eyes, jot down whatever thoughts or ideas came up for you. This is a great exercise to identify the messages that are coming from your Higher Self, and the thoughts or ideas you may tell yourself because it's what you *want* to believe (ego).

What the ego wants to think and believe can be *very* different from the actual event or information that is true. Acknowledge the truth of your own experience (subconscious versus conscious mind) by allowing your thoughts to drift and come back, again. By jotting down your immediate deep inner realizations or understandings, you will soon develop a smooth relationship between recognizing what is real versus what is illusory, or as Buddha recognizes, self-grasping. It is too easy to become overwhelmed with emotions that we (wrongly) convince ourselves are justified by facts. Get to know the real-life authentic, existing, *you*!

Finally, *accept, welcome,* and *let go*. Acknowledge that your subconscious mind always holds on to beliefs and conceptions based purely on the Self. Our subconscious mind is constantly collecting information that it thinks is best for *itself*. As our mind is flooded with judgments, conclusions, and rationales about what the ego deems best, we are constantly being challenged to always see, think and know what is true for us, through our senses. Because there is this duality between mind and body, it is important to understand the root of where all thoughts, beliefs, and desires come from, to establish unity.

There always is an inner core belief that causes one to repeat, experience, and revisit old patterns from childhood, even if most are unaware of this phenomenon. In this phase, we acknowledge where the thoughts and patterns that we've outgrown stem from. When it is in the will of our soul to let go of these old patterns, the constitution of the mind, body, and spirit will change. This is why we have to have those awkward but completely necessary conversations with ourselves! Rule out what other people think the truth is for YOU. What is *your* truth? Become present and rise up to the occasion. It's time to start filling your mind with new, supportive, uplifting, and loving thoughts!

CHAPTER FORTY-FIVE

Hand on Heart

The thirteenth-century poet Rumi once said, "The cure for pain is in the pain." At one point in my life, I found myself clamming up and becoming defensive when I first heard this quote. Now, after discovering how to feel myself again, I *understand* what Rumi meant, and why I find truth in it. What so often happens to many as a result of some of our experiences and relationships is that we dabble in a fruit basket, if you will, full of an assortment of fruits with enough of everything juicy to go around. Once each fruit, or experience, is bitten into all that's left is an empty basket—with nothing in it to remind us of what had once been a beautiful gift. I like to think of this analogy as the way God intended for us to be delivered into our lives. Just as freshly picked fruit in a gift basket has been carefully gathered to be shared among all of us as One, so are *we* meant to share and be vibrant in both our physical and spiritual nature.

When we unwrap our gift basket of perfectly harvested fruit (our bodies) and take a bite of the juiciest pear or most delectable apple (our blessings), we are thankful, energized, happy, and fulfilled. However, after days, weeks, and years of overlooked opportunities, the fruit basket will have little or no value to us anymore (disappointments, sorrow). At the most, there may be a few morsels left to savor; the rest will be tossed into a pail as scraps for birds and squirrels to rummage through.

What the similarity here is, though, is that we are all our *own* fruit basket. We come into this life with youthfulness, excitement, and love. We are born with a natural instinct to survive. Over time, toxic relationships, growing pains, stress, and unhealthy habits wear down our bodies' repair system. Help is then necessary in order to wheel us back into the balanced cycle of life. Fortunately and unfortunately, in today's world, medications seem to be the immediate resolution to help restore the human body back into balance and place our minds at ease. However; we may find a more ingrained and long-lasting type of healing if we can simply learn how to help ourselves and incorporate both approaches. By learning to listen and watch our own minds and bodies, we may become more aware of the natural signals our body sends naturally, in its call for attention and proper care. Becoming more self-aware is a practice that can help you to become more cognizant of yourself. It can help bring forth realizations and guide you to take the appropriate next steps to facilitate healing and wholeness, before the symptom(s) become unmanageable.

The physical pain that one person experiences is different than the emotional or spiritual pain someone else experiences. Both suffer, whether or not our eyes are able to actually *see* the pain. When I was first diagnosed with diabetes, I wanted every doctor to give me a prescription for a cure. I wanted to follow a recipe to get back to where I used to be. Like most of us do, I dreamed of the past, holding onto the "good old days" when I had a well of seemingly unlimited energy and enthusiasm. Was it the symptoms of the disease or the diagnosis itself that made me feel a loss of love and purpose in myself? In search of finding my happiness, and after several years of staring at myself in the mirror and cringing at my medically equipped body, I knew it was time for me to start to take *myself* on. I would care for myself like I would care for a plant—nourish the soil, plant the seeds, water appropriately, and wait for the growth that would come in due time. I give credit to my teachers, Dr. Mikao Usui, Mrs. Hawyao Takata, and Dr. Chujiro Hayashi for the beautiful Reiki teachings and it's precepts, which I have learned to appreciate, welcome, and make a part of my daily practice; one of them being, "I will be kind to *myself* and to *every* living thing."

Years ago, without realizing it, because of what I had seen, heard, and felt, I didn't feel worthy of love or affection from anyone. Sadly, I saw defeat, lack, and disappointment in myself, because that's all I had known from what I had chosen to see and believe in my upbringing and early relationships. Doing the work on myself, and making a strong, authentic decision, to be *willing* to change—was what allowed me to slowly alleviate the symptoms of my self-created life and get rid of the aspects of it that I didn't want to live out and experience any longer. I decided to let go of playing the victim, stop putting pressure on myself to "fix" myself, and quit ruminating over why this had happened to me.

After a full year of shifting my blood chemistry and my "cell memory," through the healing foods I ate, I was able to shape the chemistry of how my body responds and *promote* my own healing. To my surprise, I finally understood how this diagnosis would serve me well. I was ready to acknowledge the root of its formation, creation, and manifestation from a point of view that was *me*—not my ego. I give great thanks to my teacher, Dr. Naina, who helped me to help myself with the knowledge I acquired in becoming an Ayurvedic Nutritionist and Holistic Health Counselor. From her, I was compelled even further to trust my instinct: that healing could be obtained through food. It was through my Ayurvedic studies that I gained a great inner wisdom of how to use food as a means of bringing healing and wholeness back into my body.

Day by day, as I sought to keep myself happy, I placed my hands over my heart, over my eyes, and over my pancreas. I lit a candle, with my intention to release and to finally, just let go...again and again. Within moments of hearing the music of a violin and chimes of a bell in my imagination, I felt the tears of a broken heart and dejection stream down my flushed cheeks. I would gasp for air, hardly believing the healing experience I had ignited in myself. I would watch memories cross through my mind, while I sat still, releasing one stored up emotion after the next and erasing the pains of my past. I felt the presence of my soul uniting with something greater than myself, healing and restoring me.

My intention to help myself in order to help heal others became my great calling. And so I continued getting to know the woman I was created to be through the tears of my deep cries. I felt the pain, I welcomed it, and I thanked it for being there, for it would serve as one of the greatest lessons that life has ever taught me. It is how I experience a quality of life again, by feeling and acting as though *I already am healed.*

CHAPTER FORTY-SIX

Finishing What You Start

Having Type 1 diabetes has taught me my strength and how imperative it is for me to remain consistent with who I *am*, and what I do, to live a high-quality life. I've learned how to live my life as a spiritual vessel—constantly moving, growing, and seeking information to be shaped into the woman I am meant to be. I wasn't the kid who made straight honor roll, I didn't go to medical school, and I wasn't the loud-mouth-know-it-all blabbing and trying to sell everyone on my worth. I was the wallflower. I lived my life, pre-diagnosis, like a lily sitting in a still pond, waiting to be tapped and awakened.

That tap came unexpectedly, and it woke me up like a bucket of ice being poured down my back! It enlivened something in my spirit that enabled me to grow a new root within my core self. I was invited to see and experience the world in a variety of ways—as an observer and as a doer. I was called to stand out—to be a boldfaced word in a paragraph of standard text. Inevitably, I was encouraged to become comfortable being uncomfortable.

If you begin to listen to the conversations inside your mind, you may notice that these dialogues serve to move you in unfathomable ways. Some of them, subconsciously. Silencing the mind helps us learn more about ourselves while guiding us in taking the next best steps. It is what keeps us actively pursuing what we want to pursue—dreaming of what we want to dream—being who we want to be!

When thoughts like "next steps..."—"do this now!"—or "act!" visit your state of awareness, these are messages. The Bible states in 2 Peter 1:3 that God's power "has given us everything we need for life." If we can learn to be fully present and listen to what we already *know*, we will discover how complete we *already* are. Setback, diagnosis, worry, fear, doubt, shame...all these additives don't mix well with our recipe for success. But, we may see these things as *opportunities* to step in or step up to learn the lessons we are meant to learn— those that will prove most valuable and influential in our lives. Hope, connectivity, communication, love, willingness—these are all perfect complements to a life of peace and harmony. And yes, it's *still* possible to experience the life you've always dreamed.

CHAPTER FORTY-SEVEN

Think, Feel, Heal

I once had the opportunity to work with a woman named Blair who had been practicing herbology and acupuncture at the New York College of Traditional Chinese Medicine. Acupuncture, along with chiropractic alignment, is an essential part of my healing regimen. It invites the energy centers of the body to become more aligned and filled with the life force energy that helps to strengthen the organs, blood, and tissues. While Western medicine typically treats the symptoms, Eastern medicine has more of a "whole body" view in treating not just the symptoms, but the root cause. In my journey, I continue to seek healing in mind, body, and spirit, which must include both approaches.

I made it a point to go every week, sometimes twice, while forming bonds with several of the students who treated me. Blair was my favorite for many reasons. She had a magical touch and she knew just the right time to smile or say a kind word, or calm me with her soft voice, which sort of mimicked mine. She held my hand as I lay motionless, with needles spread across my body and tears in my eyes. She looked at me and would say, "Brittany, just be happy" in her improving English. She shared stories of how I was getting healthier, stronger, and better. She could see it, feel it, know it, and hear it. My senses spoke to me, but they spoke to her, apparently, too. She could read me by paying attention to my eyes, skin, lips, and pulse, just like I had learned in my Ayurvedic studies. My pulse was stronger, my eyes were brighter, and my skin tone, finally, had left its usual pale and yellow hue. She encouraged me to be patient because the healing was happening!

Even though I still live with diabetes, the effects of this disease were leaving my body, and I *knew* it—I woke up energetic, clear-minded, happy, and peaceful—as though I knew myself, again. I have a rhythm that encourages me to be more productive with my time, my efforts, and my life. I found myself able to peacefully sleep through the night again (yay!) and let my body repair. My bowels became healthy. My mind felt sharp and clear. Not only was my body becoming healthy, but because of my feeling and appearing healthy, I began *perceiving* myself *as* healthy. This major life-changing experience within myself inspired me to want to keep learning to love and accept myself, *just as I am*.

CHAPTER FORTY-EIGHT

From the Angle of Angels

I have come to appreciate that one of the best gifts in this life is the relationship we have in building the connection to our thoughts, emotions, and feelings. I realized through my own spiritual journey that one of the most powerful abilities we have is listening, feeling, and *using* what we learn in order to allow ourselves to be guided toward fulfilling our highest potential. By hearing, seeing, thinking, and feeling what is true Divine guidance, we can live more harmoniously in our own lives and in our ever-evolving world.

Now, some people may wonder what "true" is. What makes your truth different from my truth? Well, the way to know what is true for *you* is to *listen* and *feel* what passion feels like for *you!* Where do you find and experience that absolute joyful melody in your spirit that rings through each activity, conversation, and experience in your life? What are you usually doing when you "lose track of time" because you're "in your zone?" Every living thing has its own vibration and its own truth to experience and fulfill. Think about the amount of time you spend doing *what you love*, and make more time to be in that special space.

The way I discovered my truth was, in large part, by asking for it to be revealed to me. Through prayer and connecting with my Higher Self, I was able to receive the answers that I spent much of my awake state wondering about. This connection with my Higher Power is what helps guide me forward in my life—making choices that are in alignment with my core self and my established truth. As mentioned previously, affirmations have strongly shaped and re-molded my outlook and feelings about myself. I *still* make them a practice in my life and look forward to it as a part of my daily routine. Loving, accepting, and acknowledging my true self—my soul—has allowed me to expose myself in a way that helped me become more aware of the person I really *am*.

When you get to this point of realization within yourself, and you can see your own inner light, you will see that you are not just "someone" with a name, but a very special *piece* of the whole Universe. Naturally, you may feel guided as to how *you* can be a gift to this world. You will notice that when we can be the Light for someone else, the world becomes instantly brighter, and lighter—illuminating with indescribable love, peace and joy. Everything that comes from the intention of *being* love and *sharing* love is what will create more pathways for the collective consciousness to reflect and mirror this same harmony and vibration in each of our lives and onward.

CHAPTER FORTY-NINE

Coloring My Way Home

My life with diabetes has had its ups, downs, and everything in between. I've felt so helplessly low that my blood sugar meter won't even register a number. I have felt my tongue become tasteless, numb, and lifeless. I've had highs that have reached the 400's, burping like I'm one of the dudes after a night of burgers, fries, and a few beers. I've had to pull over to the side of the road and be late to work to attend to and catch my plummeting blood sugar numbers. I've lost nights of sleep, walking with one eye closed and the other half-open to go to the bathroom, multiple times, to urinate out the sugar that has been lingering in my system. I've squirted myself with juice while trying to slurp down a juice box at 3 a.m. just to keep me alive while my body demands it's sleep. But the point is, no matter what I've had to do, I am still *here,* still going, still growing, still learning, and still loving myself more and more for all that I have overcome. I know that by taking care of *myself*, I feel my best, and only then can I take care of others. I've learned that it doesn't matter what I've had to do—because I'm doing it. My worth is not less because of the things I have to do to keep me healthy. I've discovered I am *more than enough* simply *because* of all that I do! It is a reminder of just how strong I *am!*

No matter what obstacle, challenging circumstance, or diagnosis you may be dealing with, this book was written to let you know that *you're not alone.* I wrote this book to be a living testament that whether you have had a disease for several years and are set in your ways, or you've just been diagnosed and don't know where life may lead because of it, happiness truly is possible, if you believe—if you *believe* that there was a Divine purpose for the setback entering your life. Although, a diagnosis of a chronic condition is absolutely pit-of-the-stomach, gut-wrenchingly painful to look at, by acknowledging and accepting it as a pivotal point that calls us to look at our true selves in the mirror, one can help deter feelings of loss and inadequacy. It is a call to know and love ourselves, beyond what we have experienced. It is a call to connect and find our way back home...to ourselves and to this world!

Expressing gratitude and remaining in faith, giving thanks for all that you *are* and all that you *have,* is a beautiful way to show respect to the Universe for the love and care that is being brought to you and through you. It empowers you to stay in a positive frame of mind, feel well, and therefore; allow your body to heal—no matter what the diagnosis! Of course, no one wants to have to abide by strict regimens or feel like it's work just to be alive—but when you can shift your *mindset*, you can shift your *life*! Practicing forgiveness toward oneself and toward others is another simple way to create space within your mind-body and make room for your Higher Self to emerge. Think about how fortunate you are to *have* a body to take care of! You *have* the invitation already to *still* love yourself...despite being tested not to. Will you choose to try? Will you give yourself that chance? Are you willing and ready to rise above it? By being accountable for your own life choices, you can have the freedom and the knowledge you need to live the life you've always dreamed.

What I want you to ask your true self is this: What would you have, that you don't have already, if perfect health were *finally* achieved? Reflect on where you are at this moment in time, and where the projection may lie that leads you to believe that your right to happiness and healing must remain on layaway. What is the *purpose* of fighting to have it? Once you become clear on what it is that you *feel* you would have that you don't already, reflect on the activities you have completed in the previous chapters. Be observant of your mind and the habits that you have created, willingly or unwillingly, through your own thoughts. Doing so will help you to recognize the false ideas that you may have told yourself and convinced yourself, for too long.

By latching on to a distant future, you are *choosing* to live in a constant state of wishing, hoping, and dreaming, instead of fully living! Would we even come to know the value of our precious life if the fight was at all easy or non-existent? I've had to ask myself this question as I've grappled with my feelings about my auto-immune disease. Now, with new understanding and inner wisdom, you too can allow yourself to experience the feeling of *letting go*.

Illusions can be quite onerous because they convince us that happiness in the here and now is unattainable. Many tend to *think* that *if* they have perfect health, *then* they will be happy. Happiness is then placed in the distant future, and so every action, interaction, and thought is created based on the notion that they have to keep working for it to get there. When this happens, an invisible bubble is created which lends the wrongful idea that happiness is not available or accessible now; so, it is unattainable until the "problem" or diagnosis is fixed. Instead, we must recognize that happiness must come from *within*—and not by changing, fixing, or trying to negate one's very own self.

Disease is quite literally a dis-ease of the mind, body, and spirit. If you ignore any part of the emotional-physical-spiritual body balance, you will likely experience feelings of drainage, lethargy, or discontentment as your body attempts to bring itself back into a state of balance. It is *just as important* to do the "self-work," such as taking a quiet walk in nature or laughing along at a silly movie with family and friends as it is to occupy our mind with "real" work. Our bodies and our mind are equipped to do both—and it is up to *us* to learn how to care for each part of our soul creation.

The physical body is a vessel for the spirit that lies within each one of us...and by ignoring the emotional-physical-spiritual body *balance*, it would only be natural for the feelings we experience to be sent out as *signals* for its attention and care. By creating and maintaining a healthy mind-body connection, harmony will find *us*, instead of *us* trying to find *it*. Just as certain cars need premium oil instead of regular oil to run properly, we must give our bodies what it needs. We must supply our bodies with the right kind of food, activity, and self-care. Each body, like each vehicle, has a different license plate number. Not *one* is the same as any other. Our bodies must be designed with the intelligence that our soul has.

I'll give you an example. Before I started on my journey, I was eating pretty much whatever I felt like eating. Although I found myself quite the healthy eater (or so I thought), fruits, vegetables, any kind of meat, grains, fats, packaged foods, canned foods—you name it, I ate it. I didn't really pay attention to the way I felt *after* eating because, well, why would that matter? I paid attention to how I felt *while* I was eating—of course! I did this for years until I decided to become a vegetarian. As a *flexible* vegetarian for three years, I enjoyed lots of greens, veggies, and more green veggies. I eliminated all meat and got my protein from nuts, beans, fish, and a couple of eggs here and there. My diet was pretty predictable, and I steered clear of anything that wasn't on my "safe" list. Knowing better and wanting more for myself, I became interested in understanding where *we* all began.

I began studying the laws of the Universe, because if I had learned anything, it was that I needed to go back to the beginning. At first, I focused especially on the Law of Oneness, the Law of Action, and the Law of Cause and Effect. I knew that I must understand how I got *here* before I could fix anything about myself or my real-life experience. Then, I expanded on each law as I became more familiar with them and living, according to each law, felt harmonic and right. I began eating the colors of the rainbow, just as I would bring healing and envision the colors of my energy fields when I performed Reiki. I made sure to eat from every color group, every day, and even created a mini spreadsheet to document my eating patterns. Within days, my energy started to increase, and I began feeling much more energized and purposeful in my daily endeavors. My ideas were becoming sharp again, my mind clear, light, and happy. I even started to eat meat again—chicken, beef, turkey, just enough to keep my strength up.

Soon, my friends and family noticed, as I gained a healthy dose of confidence and regained my womanly shape. They asked me what I was doing, and I shared it with them—I was incorporating my knowledge of the chakras, or energy centers of the body, and providing the proper foods to go along with each energy center. I started using my knowledge of holistic healing, yoga, and mindfulness to bring *myself* back to wholeness. For starters, I used blue foods, like blueberries, to correlate with my throat chakra and in helping to heal my thyroid, while oranges and winter squash soothed my sacral chakra, responsible for emotions and feelings. When I desired to feel more grounded, red fruits, kidney beans and cooked apples helped me to feel a sense of connection to the Earth. I continued to use my inner voice, my Ayurvedic nutritional studies, and my intuition to know, feel, and experience the effects of food and their healing properties on my body.

Food has a different meaning to me now. Since the beginning of my healing journey, I have completely healed my thyroid, despite the number of people who told me it wasn't possible. My A1C level (a marker of how well diabetes has been controlled for a three-month period) is the lowest it has ever been at 5.8! Not only did I start to believe that I was healing, I *am* healing. I am *becoming* the woman I want and need to be. I made a way for myself, even when others tried to doubt me. By fighting for balance and making it my *absolute* mission to continue the practice of self-love, accountability and forgiveness in my daily life, I *became* healthy. I *became* healed.

Though I am still on insulin, my need for it has significantly decreased to 1/3 of what I started using when I first got diagnosed. My sensor target range had previously ranged with about 60% control. I am pleased that I am now living with 80% tighter glucose control. That measly 20%? I'll let Universe handle the rest. It is clear that because my body has *accepted* my healing desire, due to my continued belief that healing is possible, naturally, I now require less insulin. Talk about *that* for a phenomenon! This was not an overnight miracle, but it proves the power of the mind—when it's ready, the body will do what the mind tells it.

My mind has made its decision: I *am* ready to heal! I trust that with patience, love, and gratitude, if it's meant for me to be off insulin, great! But, I have *already* taken my power back! I have re-claimed my victory because I've learned *how* to truly, fully and completely love myself. Diabetes is something I have... but, it will never be who I *am*. Today, I accept *it!* I embrace *it!* But, I also respectfully and lovingly welcome it to leave, if and when, of course, it is ready to leave. And if it's not in this lifetime, well, then, I am grateful for *everything* that this diagnosis continues to teach me about my own strength and resilience. For that, I could never demand, never hate, and never express disappointment for the avenue my body chose to take to teach me the lessons *I* needed to learn. I've already learned what's driving the vehicle, and it's not my bones, muscles, and other tissues—it's God, working through me and within *me!*

My diabetes symptoms were silently draining me. I learned, observed, and watched, and when I understood enough, I began to act, think, and do better. Now that my symptoms are astonishingly lessening, my life continues to come full circle. I understand the power of *thoughts.* I know there is *so* much more healing, *so* much more life, and *so* much more love to give and go around! I *know* that this same miracle that has become my living reality—peace and harmony, beyond a diagnosis, can be true for so many whom, like myself, had no hope, or had unexpectedly lost it along the way.

Through this life of change, uncertainty, and unpredictability,

I've become stronger than I ever saw myself becoming. I have gained a type of strength that only I can attest to, from where I have been to who I am today. I've come to love myself for being as flexible as I have been—so fearless and trusting of what is to be. Maybe the long wait to find a cure will come, in the right time and space, if Universe would have it. But, maybe the cure is being *secure* in who we are as human beings, individuals, in breath, body and mind. Maybe, just as the sun and moon rise and set, just as they are meant to—and the flowers bloom and wither off, when they are meant to, *we* are meant to change, grow, and evolve, *just as we are meant to*. Could it be our resilience and beauty shine brightest when we find inner joy in our snowstorms, as well as in our favorite songs?

What if the possibility of some life-changing cure isn't in a medical lab but rather in how we handle *our* own thoughts and *our* own heart? I believe our "cure" is how we own and bring to light the fullness of our *being*, bringing peace and purpose to the forefront windows of our mind. I have come to believe that the responsibility for our healing lies in our own hearts, our relationships, and most importantly in *ourselves*. Because of the liberation that I've experienced through my own journey, I couldn't help but gather and share my experience of growth, transformation and insight, as it has led to my own self-discovery and understanding of my life purpose.

My hope is that *all* can learn of our true abilities to live more happily, peacefully and purposefully through expressing and sharing our gratitude for what *is*. We are *all* enough—perfectly created and designed, whole and complete, worthy and beautiful, just as we *are*. It is up to you, now to see and know *yourself*, as Universe always will, with Divine love and Divine trust.

This experience of living life, understanding setback, and turning it into a setup was a choice I made. It was a way for me to understand my role in my life and my body. It has taught me to slow down, to appreciate the gentle beauty in simplicity, and to be thankful for things I *can* see and things I *cannot* see. From one lesson to the next, we evolve, striving to be the best versions of ourselves in whatever we do, whatever that may look like for each of us, as we play our parts here on this Earth.

The mere act of surrendering to the larger Presence that has created this Universe will invite *you* to appreciate the abundance of possibilities and miracles just waiting for *you*, in your life! There is a certain wisdom that comes when you recognize this deeper truth. We are simply borrowing time—finding time, making time, to *be* on time—to learn what we must learn and evolve into the highest and best version of our soul-created selves.

We each share the Light in our own way, allowing it to shine wherever we go, with whomever we share our time. When we are satisfied with ourselves and create meaningful, purposeful lives, to *be* a blessing—not just receive them—this is one of the greatest gifts one can experience. Our Light is a timeless gift that is shared with everyone we encounter. The extent to which you give, receive, and honor that Light is up to you. Use it well, and learn to let go of that which is no longer serving you and your highest purpose. By loosening our tight grip and letting go, we are fully able to open our heart and our spirit to healing

I know that if I can share what I've learned from my own experience and bring insight to one's own healing abilities, you can do it, too! Begin by being your own best teacher: learn to love yourself, truly, wholly, entirely, and organically. It is when you realize *who you are* that you can become humbled by *all* that you are, and live the life you've always dreamed of. It's when you open the window to your soul that you become open, accepting, and involved with life and be of service to the world, in ways you only imagined.

I believe that self-love is the key to unlocking your truth and becoming all that you are meant to be—perfect, *exactly* the way you are. Enjoy the journey, watch and feel yourself grow, and experience the beauty in life's detours, as there is *always* a reason for them. Finding ourselves is an important part of our life's work—transcendental, curative, powerful, and worthwhile.

Embrace your own rhythm, tame your own tide, and blow with the sway of the wind in the trees! This beautiful short life begins again with one simple thought, intention, and unyielding faith that what's meant for you *will be yours!* Trust this process and know that Universe loves the person you *are*! And so, what's next, you may ask? Well, I invite *you* to sign by your own X! (Only WILLINGLY!)

Welcome to the power of Today.

Love and peaceful pieces,

Brittany Hines

Acknowledgments

This project could never have come to its fruition without the inspiration, guidance, support, teachings, and love of those who have helped me along my path. A giant thank you to my editor, Liz Seif, for helping me during this process to make every bit of my intended language flow seamlessly and harmoniously. Thank you to my teachers, especially Jagpreet Kaur, Stacey Lynn Avidane, Tina Conroy, and Theresa Banks, for helping me to find, know, love, and honor the woman I *AM*. Thank you for guiding me to recognize my own inner light and leading me to understand my crystal-clear role in this macrocosm of life and fulfill it!

Thank you to my doctors, especially, Dr. Barry Schuval, Dr. Mona Lee-Yuan, Dr. Robert Drell, and Dr. Elvira Gellis. Without you, I would never have known what it feels like to be whole again. Thank you for your top-of-the-line care, your dedication, and your willingness to help me, and for sharing your heart with mine beyond business hours. The world needs more people like you. I am forever grateful!

My family and my dear friends, I thank you with everything that I am for helping me to finally spread my wings—you have taught me the greatest gift of learning to believe in myself.

Love always,
Brittany

Am I Still Beautiful?

Am I still beautiful, with my tubing and tape? Glued to my body—
wish I could escape.
Am I still beautiful, with my computer-like device? Swung around
my hip, jolting left and right.
Do you think I'm still beautiful, despite glassy eyes? I'm sorry,
don't mind me; I was up all night.
My sensor is beeping, vibrating with such size...please, don't
laugh and poke jokes, as it saves my life.
"Can you take off your machinery?"
I can't believe he just said that to me! "Sure," I say...put my
heartbeat on hold,
Ignoring intuition, just to feel like gold.
As I plug and unplug, paving my way...
I've learned who I'll trust: Myself—every day.
I will not ask you to console my shattered heart,
for I know I am strong, though once broken; I've pressed "Start."
Watch me as I stride through my life,
Striking happiness by bringing others to Light.
I will not give up, not once; never again,
My soul runs deep, and I'll prove it fervent!
Watch me fall to my knees, embracing my Creator,
And His purpose for me.
Rising above, standing tall—pancreas on hip, needles and all.
I AM beautiful, so she said...
...she finally listened, breathed deeply,
"I won't surrender to you, diabetes, ever again."

Brittany Hines

The Rice Cake

Delicately tiptoeing across the floor,
It's three in the morning, but I need more.
One eye shut, left foot stepping front,
waiting to reach something like a sugar-laden donut.
In a rut, but the world sleeps at rest,
Alone to the kitchen to catch my fix,
My tongue is numb, pulsing for sugar to thrive,
Diabetes is in my blood and the dream is alive!

I chew as I stand in the dark, alone...
Imagining the world sleeping peacefully, in perfect tone.
Crumble, crumble, crumble...
That's what the rice cake said,
Or, maybe that's my imagination, trying to capture peace, once again.

I open my mouth wide just to get the carb load in,
Missing bits and pieces, fearing against the clock,
Time is of the essence, but where would I be if there was no "tick"; could there be a "tock?"
Back and forth as the pendulum goes,
Waiting for the rise in which I can feel as the woman I know.

Loose flowy pajamas swing at my feet,
as the bare kitchen floor grasps my toes.
I feel every particle of energy that is alive—from my being to surroundings, all feelings sensitized.
"This rice cake is round, like the globe that I know..."
Feeling crumble after crumble,
"Oh no! Did I just stub my toe?"
Irrational, delusional thoughts flood the mind,
As I strive to control what goes on inside.
"Please make me feel well again..."

Prayer becomes my answer; pen runs out of ink,
I'll walk back upstairs, I think, I think, I think.

To my bed, I lie, waiting for physical body and mind to sync,
Like an iPod just waiting for its newest update release.
I feel safe as I feel the "kick in" begin,
I know just in rush,
But, it's time to punch,
Click, click, click
And I've clocked in.

Brittany Hines